「通古察今」系列丛书

保守抑或包容
——罗马文化再求证

倪滕达 著

河南人民出版社

图书在版编目(CIP)数据

保守抑或包容：罗马文化再求证 / 倪滕达著. ——郑州：河南人民出版社，2019.12(2025.3重印)
("通古察今"系列丛书)
ISBN 978-7-215-12037-2

Ⅰ.①保… Ⅱ.①倪… Ⅲ.①文化史-研究-古罗马 Ⅳ.①K126

中国版本图书馆CIP数据核字(2019)第270874号

河南人民出版社 出版发行

(地址：郑州市郑东新区祥盛街27号 邮政编码：450016 电话：0371-65788077)
新华书店经销　　　环球东方(北京)印务有限公司印刷
开本　787mm×1092mm　　1/32　　印张　6.125
字数　82千
2019年12月第1版　　　　2025年3月第2次印刷

定价：52.00元

"通古察今"系列丛书编辑委员会

顾　问　刘家和　瞿林东　郑师渠　晁福林
主　任　杨共乐
副主任　李　帆
委　员　(按姓氏拼音排序)
　　　　　安　然　陈　涛　董立河　杜水生　郭家宏
　　　　　侯树栋　黄国辉　姜海军　李　渊　刘林海
　　　　　罗新慧　毛瑞方　宁　欣　庞冠群　吴　琼
　　　　　张　皓　张建华　张　升　张　越　赵　贞
　　　　　郑　林　周文玖

序　言

在北京师范大学的百余年发展历程中，历史学科始终占有重要地位。经过几代人的不懈努力，今天的北京师范大学历史学院业已成为史学研究的重要基地，是国家首批博士学位一级学科授予权单位，拥有国家重点学科、博士后流动站、教育部人文社会科学重点研究基地等一系列学术平台，综合实力居全国高校历史学科前列。目前被列入国家一流大学一流学科建设行列，正在向世界一流学科迈进。在教学方面，历史学院的课程改革、教材编纂、教书育人，都取得了显著的成绩，曾荣获国家教学改革成果一等奖。在科学研究方面，同样取得了令人瞩目的成就，在出版了由白寿彝教授任总主编、被学术界誉为"20世纪中国史学的压轴之作"的多卷本《中国通史》后，一批底蕴深厚、质量高超的学术论著相继问世，如八卷本《中国文化发展史》、二十卷本"中国古代社会和政治研究丛书"、三卷本《清代理学史》、五卷本《历史文化认同与中国统一多民族国家》、二十三卷本《陈垣全集》，

保守抑或包容

以及《历史视野下的中华民族精神》《中西古代历史、史学与理论比较研究》《上博简〈诗论〉研究》等,这些著作皆声誉卓著,在学界产生较大影响,得到同行普遍好评。

除上述著作外,历史学院的教师们潜心学术,以探索精神攻关,又陆续取得了众多具有原创性的成果,在历史学各分支学科的研究上连创佳绩,始终处在学科前沿。为了集中展示历史学院的这些探索性成果,我们组织编写了这套"通古察今"系列丛书。丛书所收著作多以问题为导向,集中解决古今中外历史上值得关注的重要学术问题,篇幅虽小,然问题意识明显,学术视野尤为开阔。希冀它的出版,在促进北京师范大学历史学科更好发展的同时,为学术界乃至全社会贡献一批真正立得住的学术佳作。

当然,作为探索性的系列丛书,不成熟乃至疏漏之处在所难免,还望学界同人不吝赐教。

北京师范大学历史学院
北京师范大学史学理论与史学史研究中心
北京师范大学"通古察今"系列丛书编辑委员会
2019年1月

目　录

前　言 \ 1

一、罗马早期戏剧中的希腊文化元素 \ 5

（一）大量模仿希腊剧本 \ 5

（二）广泛吸纳希腊元素 \ 21

参考资料 \ 30

二、罗马早期戏剧的本土化 \ 32

（一）创新剧本内容 \ 33

（二）探索新发展道路 \ 36

（三）推进理论发展 \ 42

参考资料 \ 47

三、历史学对修辞学的偏见 \ 49

参考资料 \ 70

四、罗马与东汉宗教批判思想之比较
——以琉善、王充为例 \ 74

（一）思想专制之论争 \ 74

（二）王充与琉善的宗教批判 \ 78

（三）弃用不等于迫害 \ 98

参考资料 \ 111

附 录

Intellectual Liberty during the Han Dynasty:
A Comparative Study of the Religious Criticism of Lucian and Wang Chong \ 119

Bibliography \ 179

前　言

　　谈到古罗马文化发展的历史，人们可能会想到首个在罗马被推上剧作家宝座的希腊俘虏李维乌斯·安德罗尼库斯（Livius Andronicus），敢于打破传统的西庇阿·阿非利加努斯（Publius Cornelius Scipio Africanus Maior），热爱希腊文学的西庇阿·阿米利安努斯（Scipio Aemilianus），用希腊文写作的哲学家元首马尔库斯·奥勒里乌斯，或者是源于伊特鲁里亚却风靡整个罗马世界的角斗士表演，活跃在罗马舞台上的荷马英雄——阿加门农、阿喀琉斯等，这些积极吸收外来文化的表现，从而认为罗马文化具有包容性。也有人会想到对广为流行的希腊事物极为排斥的、保守古板的老加图（Marcus Porcius Cato），抵制希腊文化冲击、提倡在写作时使用拉丁文的剧作家盖尤斯·卢基利乌斯（Gaius

Lucilius），明确主张恢复罗马传统的奥古斯都，以及诸多不断赞美早年间美好时光（the good old days）的伟大作家，如尤文纳里斯（Decimus Junius Juvenalis）、塞涅卡（Lucius Annaeus Seneca）、小普林尼（Gaius Plinius Caecilius Secundus）、塔西佗（Gaius Cornelius Tacitus）、西塞罗（Marcus Tullius Cicero）等，由此觉得罗马文化具有保守念旧的特点。

事实上，探究一种文化是保守，还是包容，要从多个层面、不同角度入手。这种保守或包容，从文化交流的角度讲，是对待外来文化影响的态度；从思想空间的角度讲，是文化的探索和实践所拥有的自由程度；从学科发展的角度讲，是与其他学科的排斥与交融；等等。本书就是从上述各个角度再次思考这一问题，看到古代罗马文化兼具保守和包容的特性。罗马早期戏剧的产生和发展，反映出罗马既对希腊文化积极吸收、利用，又坚持保有本土的发展特色。以罗马世界的学者为核心展开的对历史学与修辞学之间关系的探讨，展现了历史学科自我认知的过程，也是对修辞学既包容又排斥的过程。而以琉善和王充为例进行的罗马与东汉宗教批判思想的比较，在探讨古代东方文人的思想空间的同时，也再次反思了在传统宗教与政治深刻交融的二世纪罗马帝国，知识分子在文化探索和实践中享受到的自由和包容。

本书内容是我在上一阶段的古罗马史研究中，逐步积累的部分成果。由于这几篇文章都涉及罗马人对文化的探索和实践，故在此形成一个系列，组合成书，以期对罗马文化的发展特色进行再次求证。书中《罗马早期戏剧中的希腊文化元素》和《历史学对修辞学的偏见》两篇文章已在广受学界好评的核心学术期刊上发表。现在对它们重新审核，发现其中很多研究对于探究古代罗马文化的发展特点，具有较高的学术价值，故对之修订完善后收录于此。附录中的英文论文"Intellectual Liberty during the Han Dynasty：A Comparative Study of the Religious Criticism of Lucian and Wang Chong"，已在国内世界史领域的重要英文期刊 *World History Studies*（《世界史研究》）上发表。此文是在本书第四篇文章《罗马与东汉宗教批判思想之比较——以琉善、王充为例》的基础上，进一步扩充和深化后完成的，较之更为完善，因而收入附录以做参考。

本书的诞生要感谢我的老师们。我要向多年来所有对我悉心指导、鞭策教育，教我踏实治学、从史料出发、重视理论思辨的各位先生和老师，奉上最诚挚的谢意。学术研究是一条没有止境的道路，现在的成果只能代表往昔的脚印。我衷心希望本书出版后，能够得到读者善意的批评，帮助我在未来求索的道路上更进一步。

一、罗马早期戏剧中的希腊文化元素

罗马文化与希腊文化之间的关系，一直是国内外学界高度关注的问题，但因材料少而分散，故很少有人对此进行详细、具体的研究。本文力图以罗马戏剧为突破点，细致缕析罗马早期戏剧中的希腊文化元素，考察希腊文化对罗马戏剧的影响。

（一）大量模仿希腊剧本

古罗马早期戏剧多模仿、改编自希腊戏剧。在罗马早期戏剧中，希腊剧本的影子随处可见。李维乌斯·安得罗尼库斯（Livius Andronicus）、奈维乌斯（Naevius）、帕库维乌斯（Pacuvius）和阿克齐乌斯

（Accius）是罗马早期剧作家的代表。我们可以通过他们留下的戏剧断片，研究希腊文化在罗马早期戏剧中留下的痕迹。

罗马悲剧诞生初期多亦步亦趋地模仿希腊悲剧。很多作品都能找出其仿效的原型。例如，李维乌斯的《持鞭者埃阿斯》(*Aiax Mastigophorus*)与索福克勒斯的《埃阿斯》(*Αἴας*)情节设置十分相似；[1] 奈维乌斯的《伊菲革涅亚》(*Iphigenia*)一定程度上参照了欧里庇得斯的《伊菲革涅亚在陶里克人中》(*Ἰφιγ. ἡ ἐν Ταύροις*)；[2]《吕枯耳戈斯》(*Lycurgus*)则是仿照埃斯库罗斯的名为《吕枯耳癸亚》(*Λυκουργεία*)的三部曲写成；[3] 帕库维乌斯的作品《关于兵器的判决》(*Armorum Iudicium*)基本取材于埃斯库罗斯的《关于兵器的评判》(*Ὅπλων Κρίσις*)，个别地方取自阿克提努斯（Arctinus）的作品；[4]《克律塞斯》(*Chryses*)的标题本身就说明其故事

---

[1] *Remains of Old Latin* II (*Livius, Naevius, Pacuvius, Accius*), Loeb Classical Library, Cambridge, Massachusetts: Harvard University Press, first printed 1936, p. 7.

[2] *Remains of Old Latin* II (*Livius, Naevius, Pacuvius, Accius*), p. 121.

[3] *Remains of Old Latin* II (*Livius, Naevius, Pacuvius, Accius*), p. 123.

[4] *Remains of Old Latin* II (*Livius, Naevius, Pacuvius, Accius*), p. 172.

原型为索福克勒斯的《克律塞斯》(Χρύσης),不过其第107至第115行的内容说明它也参考了欧里庇得斯的《克律斯珀斯》(Χρύσιππος),并且部分材料取自《伊菲革涅亚在陶里克人中》;[1]《赫尔弥奥娜》(Hermiona)模仿的应该是索福克勒斯的《赫尔弥奥涅》(Ἑρμιόνη)[2];阿克齐乌斯的《阿尔克迈翁》(Alcmeo)是根据欧里庇得斯的《阿尔克迈翁过科林斯》(Ἀλκμαίων διὰ Κορίνθου)改编的。[3] 同帕库维乌斯一样,阿克齐乌斯也写了《关于兵器的判决》(Armorum Iudicium),不过很显然他模仿的是欧里庇得斯和索福克勒斯的作品,而非埃斯库罗斯的。[4] 此外,阿克齐乌斯的《阿特柔斯》(Atreus)学习了索福克勒斯的剧作,但其中有两段残篇模仿的是欧里庇得斯的作品;[5]而他的《后辈》(Epigoni)是以索福克勒斯的《后代》(Ἐπίγονοι)为基础写成的。[6] 经统计,李维乌斯、奈维乌斯、帕库

---

[1] *Remains of Old Latin* II (*Livius*, *Naevius*, *Pacuvius*, *Accius*), p. 193.
[2] *Remains of Old Latin* II (*Livius*, *Naevius*, *Pacuvius*, *Accius*), p. 225.
[3] *Remains of Old Latin* II (*Livius*, *Naevius*, *Pacuvius*, *Accius*), p. 332.
[4] *Remains of Old Latin* II (*Livius*, *Naevius*, *Pacuvius*, *Accius*), p. 358.
[5] *Remains of Old Latin* II (*Livius*, *Naevius*, *Pacuvius*, *Accius*), p. 381.
[6] *Remains of Old Latin* II (*Livius*, *Naevius*, *Pacuvius*, *Accius*), p. 420.

维乌斯和阿克齐乌斯留下来的悲剧残篇总共七十五篇，其中可以推断出模仿对象的有三十八篇，占总数量的一半以上。这充分说明了罗马早期悲剧师从希腊。

罗马早期剧作家在学习希腊戏剧过程中，在情节设置和对白内容上都细致地模仿希腊剧本。[1] 上述四位作家留下的作品断片中，在具体语言和情节上几乎照搬希腊作品的有二十四段。其中，阿克齐乌斯留下的作品最多，借鉴希腊戏剧的数量最大，模仿痕迹也最重。以其《酒神的信徒》(*Bacchae*)和《腓尼基妇女》(*Phoenissae*)为例，《酒神的信徒》留下断片十八段，其中在情节和语言上与欧里庇得斯的悲剧《酒神的伴侣》(*βάκχαι*)雷同者有八段；《腓尼基妇女》共留下断片十三段，其中在情节和语言上与欧里庇得斯的《腓尼基妇女》(*Φοίνισσαι*)相似者有五段。在

---

[1] 为进一步研究这些戏剧残篇究竟在何种程度上模仿了希腊剧本，并探求其模仿方式，笔者将上述作家现存的残篇与希腊戏剧进行了逐句比对。遗憾的是，希腊戏剧佚失严重，很多重要作品现已无法找到。目前，古希腊所有存世的悲剧仅 32 部。因此在研究过程中，只能将上述四位剧作家的作品残篇同现存的古希腊戏剧进行比较。本文使用的古罗马早期戏剧残篇均出自《洛布古典丛书》的英译本，用来比对的完整的希腊戏剧出自《古希腊悲剧喜剧全集》。

《酒神的信徒》中,特瑞西阿斯赞美狄俄尼索斯时说:"因为一个人没有办法说出,或创造出足以与其伟大相配的辞藻。"[1]在欧里庇得斯的悲剧《酒神的伴侣》中,特瑞西阿斯在向彭透斯赞美酒神时,也说了类似的话:"你所讥笑的这位新神,我没法说出,他在全希腊将有多么伟大。"[2]另外,在《酒神的信徒》中,当狄俄尼索斯被绑着带到彭透斯面前时,卫兵说:"他在那时那地显现自己,而且礼貌地微笑,出于自愿地,出现在我们这些吃惊的人面前。"[3]而在《酒神的伴侣》中,同样的情节下,卫队长说:"他束手就擒,没有拔腿逃跑,酒红的脸色没有改变,没有发白,而是笑着叫我们把他绑了带走,他等在那里,使我们毫不费事。"[4]在阿克齐乌斯的作品中,彭透斯嘲弄地夸奖被俘的酒神时说:"你的外表和形象很整洁啊,陌

---

[1] *Remains of Old Latin* II (*Livius*,*Naevius*,*Pacuvius*,*Accius*), p. 397.
[2] 〔古希腊〕埃斯库罗斯等:《古希腊悲剧喜剧全集》第5卷,张竹明、王焕生译,南京:译林出版社,2007,第228页。
[3] *Remains of Old Latin* II (*Livius*,*Naevius*,*Pacuvius*,*Accius*), p. 399.
[4] 〔古希腊〕埃斯库罗斯等:《古希腊悲剧喜剧全集》第5卷,第235—236页。

生人。"[1]而在《酒神的伴侣》中,彭透斯说:"客人啊,你人材不难看,很能讨女人喜欢。"[2]此外,阿克齐乌斯笔下的报信人在描述酒神的信徒们如何喂动物吃奶时说:"很不优雅地哺育其他物种的幼仔。"[3]《酒神的伴侣》中则有这样的表达:"报信人甲:有的人把小鹿和野生的狼仔抱在怀里,喂它们白色的奶。"[4]在《酒神的信徒》中,报信人转述彭透斯的话说:"某棵松树的树干或高耸的……"[5]而在《酒神的伴侣》中,同样是报信人转述道:"……爬到岩石上或高高的松树上……"[6]

我们可以通过表格更加清晰地看到二者的相似之处:

---

[1] *Remains of Old Latin* Ⅱ (*Livius*, *Naevius*, *Pacuvius*, *Accius*), p. 399.
[2] 〔古希腊〕埃斯库罗斯等:《古希腊悲剧喜剧全集》第5卷,第236页。
[3] *Remains of Old Latin* Ⅱ (*Livius*, *Naevius*, *Pacuvius*, *Accius*), p. 401.
[4] 〔古希腊〕埃斯库罗斯等:《古希腊悲剧喜剧全集》第5卷,第254页。
[5] *Remains of Old Latin* Ⅱ (*Livius*, *Naevius*, *Pacuvius*, *Accius*), p. 401.
[6] 〔古希腊〕埃斯库罗斯等:《古希腊悲剧喜剧全集》第5卷,第279页。

一、罗马早期戏剧中的希腊文化元素

表1 阿克齐乌斯的《酒神的信徒》与欧里庇得斯的《酒神的伴侣》对比表

罗马	希腊
《酒神的信徒》 阿克齐乌斯 著	《酒神的伴侣》 欧里庇得斯 著
特瑞西阿斯：因为一个人没有办法说出，或创造出足以与其伟大相配的辞藻。	特瑞西阿斯：你所讥笑的这位新神，我没法说出，他在希腊将有多么伟大。
卫兵：他在那时那地显现自己，而且礼貌地微笑，出于自愿地，出现在我们这些吃惊的人面前。	卫队长：他束手就擒，没有拔腿逃跑，酒红的脸色没有改变，没有发白，而是笑着叫我们把他绑了带走，他等在那里，使我们毫不费事。
彭透斯：你的外表和形象很整洁啊，陌生人。	彭透斯：客人啊，你人材不难看，很能讨女人喜欢。
报信人：很不优雅地哺育其他物种的幼仔。	报信人：有的人把小鹿和野生的狼仔抱在怀里，喂它们白色的奶。
报信人：某棵松树的树干或高耸的……	报信人：……爬到岩石上或高高的松树上……

通过这几段内容的对比，我们可以看到，阿克齐乌斯不仅参考了欧里庇得斯悲剧的故事情节，还模仿了其剧中角色的对白。虽然他没有一成不变地照搬，但是从二者的相似程度来看，阿克齐乌斯作品的语言只是在希腊剧本译文基础上略作调整而已。

阿克齐乌斯作品的这一特点在《腓尼基妇女》中表现得更为明显。在《腓尼基妇女》的序言中，伊奥

保守抑或包容

卡斯特在戏剧开场时说道:"噢,太阳神啊,当你炽热的战车以及闪耀着烈焰飞奔的神马在热浪中现身的时候,为什么照耀底比斯的光芒带来的是如此不祥的预兆,如此不幸的预言?"[1]在欧里庇得斯的作品《腓尼基妇女》中,也是伊奥卡斯特在说开场白:"太阳神啊,在卡德摩斯远离腓尼基海边王国来到我们这地方的那一天,你在星空中劈开一条路,驾着快马拉的镶金战车,带着万丈火焰疾驰前进的时候,你把多么不幸的光线射向了忒拜[2]呀!"[3]在阿克齐乌斯的《腓尼基妇女》中,特瑞西阿斯告知克瑞昂,为了保住这片土地,必须用一个龙牙的后代来献祭,因此一定要献出克瑞昂本人或其另一个儿子墨诺叩斯:"一个出身于龙的武士的血统者。"[4]而在欧里庇得斯的悲剧《腓尼基妇女》中,当特瑞西阿斯告诉克瑞昂必须杀死他的儿子时说:"龙齿所生的种族里必须有一个子孙被杀献。"[5]在阿克

---

[1] *Remains of Old Latin* II (*Livius*, *Naevius*, *Pacuvius*, *Accius*), p. 525.
[2] 即底比斯。
[3] 〔古希腊〕埃斯库罗斯等:《古希腊悲剧喜剧全集》第4卷,第333页。
[4] *Remains of Old Latin* II (*Livius*, *Naevius*, *Pacuvius*, *Accius*), p. 529.
[5] 〔古希腊〕埃斯库罗斯等:《古希腊悲剧喜剧全集》第4卷,第393页。

一、罗马早期戏剧中的希腊文化元素

齐乌斯的作品中,克瑞昂告诉俄狄浦斯必须离开这座城市时说:"他已经命令将你放逐到这个世界你该被放逐去的地方,以免你的过错将底比斯变成一片废墟。"[1]而在欧里庇得斯的《腓尼基妇女》中,同样的情节下,克瑞昂说:"因此我再不允许你住在这地方了。因为特瑞西阿斯说得很明白:只要你住在这地方,城邦便不会有好运。"[2](见表2)

表2 阿克齐乌斯的《腓尼基妇女》与欧里庇得斯的

《腓尼基妇女》对比表

罗马	希腊
《腓尼基妇女》 阿克齐乌斯 著	《腓尼基妇女》 欧里庇得斯 著
伊奥卡斯特:噢,太阳神啊,当炽热的战车以及闪耀着烈焰飞奔的神马在热浪中现身的时候,为什么照耀底比斯的光芒带来的是如此不祥的预兆,如此不幸的预言?	伊奥卡斯特:太阳神啊,在卡德摩斯远离腓尼基海边王国来到我们这地方的那一天,你在星空中劈开一条路,驾着快马拉的镶金战车,带着万丈火焰疾驰前进的时候,你把多么不幸的光线射向了忒拜呀!
特瑞西阿斯:一个出身于龙的武士的血统者。	特瑞西阿斯:龙齿所生的种族里必须有一个子孙被杀献。

---

[1] *Remains of Old Latin* II(*Livius*, *Naevius*, *Pacuvius*, *Accius*), p. 531.
[2] 〔古希腊〕埃斯库罗斯等:《古希腊悲剧喜剧全集》第4卷,第428页。

续表

罗马	希腊
克瑞昂：他已经命令将你放逐到这个世界你该被放逐去的地方，以免你的过错将底比斯变成一片废墟。	克瑞昂：因此我再不允许你住在这地方了。因为特瑞西阿斯说得很明白：只要你住在这地方，城邦便不会有好运。

除上面两部作品外，阿克齐乌斯的其他剧作也同样细致地模仿了希腊戏剧。例如，其《关于兵器的判决》就与索福克勒斯的《埃阿斯》十分相像。在《关于兵器的判决》中，埃阿斯对欧律萨刻斯说过这样一句话："……要像你的父亲那样英勇，但是运气上不要像他那样。"[1] 而索福克勒斯在《埃阿斯》中写的是："啊，我的孩子，愿你比父亲幸运，别的都像他。"[2]

事实上，希腊悲剧并非仅影响了阿克齐乌斯一人。很多罗马剧作家都细致地模仿希腊悲剧的语言和情节。例如，在李维乌斯的《持鞭者埃阿斯》中，透克罗斯就人们轻易忘却逝去的英雄发表评论说："美德受到了称赞，但赞美却比春天的冰冻融化得还快。"[3] 而

---

[1] *Remains of Old Latin* Ⅱ (*Livius*, *Naevius*, *Pacuvius*, *Accius*), p. 367.
[2] 〔古希腊〕埃斯库罗斯等：《古希腊悲剧喜剧全集》第2卷，第368页。
[3] *Remains of Old Latin* Ⅱ (*Livius*, *Naevius*, *Pacuvius*, *Accius*), p. 9.

一、罗马早期戏剧中的希腊文化元素

索福克勒斯的《埃阿斯》中有这样一句话:"透克罗斯:可叹啊,人一死,对他的感激消失得多快!对他的背叛也来得多快啊呀!"[1]另外,在奈维乌斯的《伊菲革涅亚》中,作家在描述一个牧人向伊菲革涅亚报告有两个年轻人到来时写道:"合唱队:来了一个驱赶着耕牛的农夫。"[2]而欧里庇得斯的《伊菲革涅亚在陶里克人中》写的是:"歌队长:看,那里从海边来了一个牧人来给你报告什么消息。"[3]可见二者内容极为相似。此外,在奈维乌斯的作品中,托阿斯命令人们追踪逃亡者时说:"你们所有居住在多瑙河沿岸和寒冷地区的人们。"[4]而欧里庇得斯悲剧中的内容则是:"托阿斯:我们这非希腊地方的全体市民们。"[5](见表3)

---

[1] 〔古希腊〕埃斯库罗斯等:《古希腊悲剧喜剧全集》第2卷,第413页。
[2] *Remains of Old Latin* II (*Livius*, *Naevius*, *Pacuvius*, *Accius*), p. 121.
[3] 〔古希腊〕埃斯库罗斯等:《古希腊悲剧喜剧全集》第3卷,第452页。
[4] *Remains of Old Latin* II (*Livius*, *Naevius*, *Pacuvius*, *Accius*), p. 123.
[5] 〔古希腊〕埃斯库罗斯等:《古希腊悲剧喜剧全集》第3卷,第534页。

表 3 上述希腊、罗马戏剧内容对比表

罗马	希腊
埃阿斯：……要像你的父亲那样英勇，但是运气上不要像他那样。（《关于兵器的判决》阿克齐乌斯著）	埃阿斯：啊，我的孩子，愿你比父亲幸运，别的都像他。（《埃阿斯》索福克勒斯著）
透克罗斯：美德受到了称赞，但赞美却比春天的冰冻融化得还快。（《持鞭者埃阿斯》李维乌斯著）	透克罗斯：叹啊，人一死，对他的感激消失得多快！对他的背叛也来得多快啊呀！（《埃阿斯》索福克勒斯著）
合唱队：来了一个驱赶着耕牛的农夫。（《伊菲革涅亚》奈维乌斯著）	歌队长：看，那里从海边来了一个牧人来给我报告什么消息。（《伊菲革涅亚在陶里克人中》欧里庇得斯著）
托阿斯：你们所有居住在多瑙河沿岸和寒冷地区的人们。（《伊菲革涅亚》奈维乌斯著）	托阿斯：我们这非希腊地方的全体市民们。（《伊菲革涅亚在陶里克人中》欧里庇得斯著）

通过将罗马早期戏剧残篇同希腊剧本进行比对可知，罗马早期悲剧深受希腊戏剧影响。罗马作家认真学习、模仿希腊剧本的语言和故事情节。事实上，希腊戏剧带来的影响并非仅限于悲剧领域，也存在于喜剧之中。李维乌斯的喜剧作品《短剑》（*Gladiolus*）这个名字就暗指一个希腊作品原型《匕首》（Ἐγχειρίδιον）。米南德（Menander）、腓力门（Philemon）和索菲鲁斯（Sophilus）均写过名为《匕

首》的作品。[1] 李维乌斯的《赌徒》(Ludius)与阿里斯托梅尼(Aristomenes)的《骗子》(Γόητες)和安菲亚斯(Amphias)的《欺骗》(Πλάνος)都十分相像;[2] 奈维乌斯的《刺穿》(Acontizomenos)应该改编自狄奥尼西奥斯(Dionysius)的《刺伤》(Ακοντιζόμενος);[3] 而其《谄媚者》(Colax)则是以米南德的《谄媚者》(Κόλαξ)为基础写成的;[4]《卖花环的女子》(Corollaria)模仿了攸布鲁斯(Eubulus)的《卖花环的人》(Στεφανοπωλίδες);[5]《疯狂》(Dementes)与迪菲鲁斯(Diphilus)的《发狂》(Μαινόμενος)十分相像;《德米特里厄斯》(Demeterius)与亚历克西斯的《重情义的德米特里厄斯》(Δημήτριος ἢ Φιλέταιρος)也颇为相似。[6]

除上述几位外,还有一位喜剧家值得关注,那就是普劳图斯(Plautus)。普劳图斯是第一位有完整作品

---

[1] *Remains of Old Latin* II (*Livius, Naevius, Pacuvius, Accius*), p. 21.
[2] *Remains of Old Latin* II (*Livius, Naevius, Pacuvius, Accius*), p. 21.
[3] *Remains of Old Latin* II (*Livius, Naevius, Pacuvius, Accius*), p. 75.
[4] *Remains of Old Latin* II (*Livius, Naevius, Pacuvius, Accius*), p. 83.
[5] *Remains of Old Latin* II (*Livius, Naevius, Pacuvius, Accius*), p. 87.
[6] *Remains of Old Latin* II (*Livius, Naevius, Pacuvius, Accius*), p. 89.

传世的罗马剧作家。[1] 他的作品也是依据希腊剧本改编而成。根据其前言或剧中内容一般可以推测出作者所模仿的希腊戏剧原本。例如，喜剧《赶驴》模仿的希腊原本是摩菲洛斯的《赶驴人》；《普修多卢斯》模仿的希腊原本是《迦太基人》（作者不详，米南德和阿勒克西得斯均有同名作品）；《行囊》模仿的希腊原本是《海船》；《吹牛的军人》模仿的希腊原本是《吹牛者》；等等。[2]

经统计，帕库维乌斯和阿克齐乌斯两位作家没有喜剧作品传世。李维乌斯留下喜剧残篇三篇，模仿的是亚历山大时代的新喜剧。[3] 奈维乌斯留下喜剧残篇较多，有二十九篇，总共包含断片六十六段（包括无法确定出处的断片四段），但其中只有《他林敦少女》（*Tarentilla*）留下残篇内容相对较多，有十一段。其他作品残篇均只留下一两段断片，每段断片多者有四五句，少的只有半句。有的作品甚至只留下了标题，内

---

[1] 王焕生：《古罗马文学史》，北京：人民文学出版社，2006，第34页。
[2] 王焕生：《古罗马文学史》，第36页。
[3] O. Szemerényi, "The Origins of Roman Drama and Greek Tragedy", *Hermes*, 103. Bd., H. 3 (1975), p. 300.

一、罗马早期戏剧中的希腊文化元素

容全部佚失。故目前只能根据《洛布古典丛书》提供的信息，总结出这二十九篇作品中，至少有八篇模仿了希腊戏剧，至于它们是如何模仿的已很难查证。可以确定的是，普劳图斯的一些作品模仿了古希腊喜剧，但对于其模仿方式及程度，同样由于材料匮乏，无从确切查考。

罗马早期戏剧大量模仿希腊作品并非偶然。在早期戏剧萌芽时，罗马正走向地中海，并在对外征服的道路上取得了一系列的胜利。在对外发展过程中，罗马人同希腊人发生了广泛的联系。丰富发达的希腊文化成为罗马人学习的榜样。于是罗马人开始大量引入希腊文化。希腊戏剧就在这一时期走进了罗马人的生活。

最先为罗马引入希腊戏剧的是意大利半岛南部的希腊殖民者。随着罗马成功地向南扩张，很多有文化的希腊人作为俘虏被带回罗马。他们多在罗马人家庭中服务，成为希腊文化影响罗马的重要媒介。罗马第一位剧作家李维乌斯就是一名希腊人，在公元前272年他林敦投降罗马后，被作为奴隶带回罗马，后教授一些富家子弟拉丁语和希腊语。李维乌斯是第一位将希腊戏剧引入罗马的作家。"罗马人在其自己的公共娱乐中没有类似的东西。当然,他们有某种舞台表演。其本土的娱乐形式是'杂戏'(satura)……希腊戏剧在这个时期展现出了前所未有的魅力,给罗马人留下了新颖而深刻的印象。公元前240年,李维乌斯将一部希腊悲剧和一部希腊喜剧翻译成拉丁语搬上罗马舞台,立刻获得了成功,并且在罗马刮起了追逐希腊风格戏剧的流行风,将陈旧的杂戏淘汰出了舞台。"[1] 从此,接下来的罗马作家们也都开始走上了翻译和模仿希腊戏剧的道路。就这样,在各种希腊文化的强力影响下,罗马戏剧以翻译希腊剧本为开端,逐渐发展起来。因此在罗马早期戏剧中,希腊剧本的影子随处可见。

综上所述,罗马剧作家在戏剧创作初期,主要学习和翻译古希腊剧本。这一特点不仅体现在古罗马早期悲剧中,而且在喜剧方面同样有迹可循。这再次证明了罗马文化具有开放性,善于吸收其他先进文明的成果是其重要特点。模仿是罗马戏剧之路的起点,为

---

[1] Edna M. Hooker, *Changing Fashions in Ancient Drama* II, *Greece & Rome*, Second Series, Vol. 7, No. 2 (Oct., 1960), published by Cambridge University Press on behalf of The Classical Association, p. 143.

随后其本土特色的彰显奠定了基础。

（二）广泛吸纳希腊元素

除剧本外，希腊文化还有很多元素从不同角度影响着古罗马早期戏剧。它们丰富了罗马戏剧的语言，激发了罗马作家的灵感，为戏剧思想的顺利表达创造了条件。文字是文化传播的重要媒介。随着希腊文化的涌入，希腊文字成为影响罗马早期戏剧的重要因素。希腊文字对古罗马戏剧的影响，主要体现在两个方面：一是拉丁文字的发展；二是戏剧内涵的丰富。

古希腊文字促进了拉丁语构词法的发展。在古罗马早期戏剧家当中，对拉丁语构词法研究最深入者当属阿克齐乌斯。他就拉丁语拼写提出了一系列新规则，其中很多都沿用了希腊文法。例如，阿克齐乌斯提出"对于软腭音 n 后面加上一个腭音的情况，有特定的表达方式。因此 ng 音应用 gg 来表示，nc 用 gc 表示。这两种方法沿袭了希腊文用法"。[1] 另外"希腊名词和

---

[1] *Remains of Old Latin* Ⅱ (*Livius*, *Naevius*, *Pacuvius*, *Accius*), p.xxii.

名字的拼写应严格保留下来"。[1] 阿克齐乌斯的一些拉丁语构词法，受到了同时代以及后世罗马人的重视，[2] 对强化拉丁语的规范性意义重大。由此可见，希腊语对拉丁文字的发展影响巨大。构词法决定了拉丁文字的书写方式，而文字是剧本的重要载体和表现工具。因此在古罗马剧本中，古希腊文的影子随处可见。

希腊文字的引入不仅改变了罗马文字，更影响到罗马戏剧的内涵。字词是语言的重要组成部分。语言是人类思维的工具。语言表达需要思维的支持，而思维运转需要通过语言来完成。众多源于希腊语的拉丁文字，在无形之中改变着罗马人的思维。拉丁语中有很多词汇来源于希腊语。这说明罗马人生活中本来没有这些词，而它们的出现是古希腊、罗马文化交流的结果。一些拉丁词汇，如果没有希腊文化的引入，很可能不会出现，也就无法在罗马戏剧中使用。是故这些词汇所代表的概念同样难以出现在罗马戏剧当中。因此，罗马剧本作为思维和语言的结合体，自然会深受希腊文字的影响。这一影响最有力的证据是，罗马

---

[1] *Remains of Old Latin* II (*Livius*, *Naevius*, *Pacuvius*, *Accius*), p. xxiii.
[2] *Remains of Old Latin* II (*Livius*, *Naevius*, *Pacuvius*, *Accius*), p. xxiv.

一、罗马早期戏剧中的希腊文化元素

剧本中存在众多以希腊文字为词源的拉丁文。

在奈维乌斯的《关于一件丘尼卡袍》(*Tunicularia*)里有这样一句话:"ecbolas aulas quassant..."(他们打碎被丢弃的罐子……),其中拉丁文"ecbolas"一词,源于希腊文"ἐκβολή"。[1] 在奈维乌斯的悲剧《吕库古》(*Lycurgus*)里有:"Diabathra in pedibus habebat, erat amictus epicroco."(他脚蹬便鞋,身披藏红花色的袍子。)这句话中的"diabathra"和"epicrocum"(即epicroco的主格)其实都是希腊文。[2] 在帕库维乌斯的作品中也有很多源于希腊文的拉丁语。其中有一篇就连标题——*DULORESTES*(《当奴隶的俄瑞斯特斯》)都是由两个希腊单词"δοῦλος"和"Ὀρέστης"组合而成的。[3] 此外,帕库维乌斯的戏剧残篇中有这样一句话:"Alcyonis ritu litus pervolgans feror."(像一只翠鸟一般,我捕猎于掠过的沙滩。)文中该鸟的拉丁语称呼是"alcedo"(即alcyonis的主格),它的希腊名字是

---

[1] *Remains of Old Latin* II (*Livius*, *Naevius*, *Pacuvius*, *Accius*), p.106.

[2] *Remains of Old Latin* II (*Livius*, *Naevius*, *Pacuvius*, *Accius*), pp. 130-131.

[3] *Remains of Old Latin* II (*Livius*, *Naevius*, *Pacuvius*, *Accius*), p. 208.

"ἀλκυών"[1]，二者拼写方式非常相近。在阿克齐乌斯的作品残篇里也有类似的例子。例如，在《菲纽斯之子》（*Phinidae*）中，菲纽斯的一个儿子在讲述伊达亚如何诬陷克里奥帕特拉时说："se venenis sterilem esse illius opera et medicina autumans."（说她是被她下毒害得不能生育。）这里"medicina"一词用于表示毒药。该用法源于希腊语。希腊人把毒药称作"φάρμακον"[2]。

上述例子表明，在古罗马早期戏剧作品中，剧作家们总是不可避免地用到一些与希腊文有关的拉丁文。当罗马戏剧中的一些概念或思想很难用当时已有的拉丁文表述清楚时，作家们便会选择使用希腊语。由此，希腊文字所代表的内涵也随之融入罗马戏剧当中。

希腊神话在推动罗马早期戏剧发展方面，同样功不可没。它们为古罗马早期戏剧提供了创作材料。依然以李维乌斯、奈维乌斯、帕库维乌斯和阿克齐乌斯

---

[1] *Remains of Old Latin* Ⅱ (*Livius*, *Naevius*, *Pacuvius*, *Accius*), pp. 314–315.

[2] *Remains of Old Latin* Ⅱ (*Livius*, *Naevius*, *Pacuvius*, *Accius*), pp. 522–523.

这四位剧作家为例。他们的悲剧作品大量取材于希腊神话故事。在古罗马早期悲剧中,李维乌斯留下的作品总共十篇(包括《奥德赛》在内);奈维乌斯有七篇(不包括历史剧);阿克齐乌斯有四十六篇。[1] 这些悲剧作品全部以希腊神话为素材。而帕库维乌斯留给我们的十四篇悲剧作品,除《保卢斯》(*Paulus*)[2] 外,也都是围绕着希腊神话故事展开的。喜剧方面也有以希腊神话为素材者。普劳图斯的喜剧《安菲特律翁》就是对希腊神话的戏拟,讲述了宙斯爱上阿尔克墨涅的故事。可见,希腊神话是罗马早期戏剧主题的重要组成部分,丰富了罗马人的舞台。

希腊神话为罗马早期戏剧所青睐有其合理性。早期作家对希腊戏剧的大量模仿,自然使得希腊神话成为罗马早期戏剧的主要素材。与此同时,希腊神话所传达的理念符合罗马当时的政治形势,受到罗马观众的欢迎。以李维乌斯为例,他在罗马生活的时间为公

---

[1] 笔者没有将阿克齐乌斯的历史剧及其他作品纳入悲剧当中。

[2] 因为《洛布古典丛书》将其放在悲剧一类中,故笔者也将其列入悲剧。至于奈维乌斯的两部历史剧《克拉斯提迪乌姆》和《罗穆路斯》(或《狼》),因《洛布古典丛书》直接指出它们是历史剧,所以笔者没有将它们算在悲剧当中。

元前272年至公元前204年——正值第二次迦太基战争时期。此时,在元老院和战场上,个人作用开始凸显出来。罗马政坛涌现出一批人才,其中就有西庇阿。在战争中,西庇阿的作用举足轻重,展现出了出众的军事才能、卓越的领导力和判断力。第二次迦太基战争期间,他在西班牙取得胜利后,完全依靠个人的力量和智慧征集了一批志愿军前往阿非利加。在西庇阿的指挥下,这支军队在阿非利加所向披靡,屡立战功。战争结束后,迦太基人意欲同罗马订立和约。"西庇阿也派人建议罗马人批准这个协议。据说,他提出这样建议,有两方面的原因:一方面,他认为和平于罗马有利;另一方面,因为他听说执政官 C. 考尼利乌斯·蓝图鲁斯(C. Cornelius Lentulus)正等着接替他的指挥权,而他不愿别人夺走终结这场战争的荣耀。总之,西庇阿吩咐他的使者说,如果罗马人有所拖延,那么他将独自缔结合约。"[1] 这反映出军功荣誉是当时罗马人的重要追求,而功勋卓著的西庇阿的个人威望和权力,足以影响整个罗马的政治决策。

---

[1] Appian, *Roman History*, Loeb Classical Library, Cambridge, Massachusetts: Harvard University Press, first printed 1912, p. 489.

一、罗马早期戏剧中的希腊文化元素

政治上个人能力的展现以及赢得肯定，使当时的罗马将军们受到个人英雄主义的鼓舞。普通民众也向成功人士投去敬佩的目光。在这样的背景下，以古希腊神话为主题的戏剧更易受到观众的追捧。因为希腊神话大多都颂扬英雄的智慧与伟大，故事中的英雄为了理想、祖国和世人的美好生活而贡献力量，做出牺牲。例如，阿喀琉斯、埃癸斯托斯和特洛伊木马的故事等，都是如此。而此时的政治家们也利用这样的理念，"为其自身创造出一种新型领袖的角色"[1]。因此，与当时罗马政坛风向相符的希腊神话，成为罗马早期戏剧的重要素材。

地域背景是罗马早期戏剧中的另一常见希腊元素。罗马戏剧经常将故事场景设置在希腊地区。罗马早期作家在编写悲剧时多模仿或翻译希腊悲剧，致使二者故事情节和角色对白相似度极高。再加上罗马戏剧家热衷于以希腊神话为素材，故而在作品中故事的发生地必然多是希腊地区。而喜剧，除模仿希腊剧本外，还多关注罗马社会现实生活，在嬉笑怒骂中针砭

---

[1] R. H. 巴洛:《罗马人》，黄韬译，上海：上海人民出版社，2000，第65页。

时弊。此时罗马虽是共和政体,公民在名义上是平等的,但政坛终归还是由贵族把持。如果戏剧作品内容针对性过于明显,就会遭到当权者的不满和打压。奈维乌斯就曾因大胆而尖锐地批判罗马当时的政治名人而受到迫害。[1] 由此可以看出,剧作家在创作过程中需要自我保护,用隐晦的手法谈论时政和社会生活。因此将场景设置在希腊,是一把很好的保护伞。如果作品涉及敏感话题,作家们就可以此来麻痹当权者而避免迫害;倘若不幸被其发觉,还可用之来为自己辩护。故罗马早期作家在创作喜剧时,也多以希腊地区为故事背景。普劳图斯就曾在《孪生兄弟》[即《两个米内克穆斯》(*Menaechmi*)]的开场词中说:"诗人们在喜剧中常常这样安排:他们把所描写的事情全都设想

---

[1] *Remains of Old Latin* II (*Livius*, *Naevius*, *Pacuvius*, *Accius*), pp. xv-xvi:奈维乌斯令塞西利乌斯·梅特鲁斯家族感到头疼,所以 Q. 塞西利乌斯·梅特鲁斯在公元前 206 年扬言要报复他。最终,"由于总是以希腊诗人的方式(也就是用"古代喜剧"的方式)侮辱和嘲笑国家的领导人",奈维乌斯在罗马被刑事三人委员会投入监狱。他在狱中写了两部戏剧——《预言者》和《利昂》,就自己的行为表示歉意,后被平民保民官释放,却随即被驱逐出罗马和意大利。这是贵族们,尤其是梅特鲁斯家族一手安排的。

发生在希腊……"[1]另外,他还说自己和其他作家不一样,故事发生在哪里就说哪里。[2]但是他的故事却也多发生在希腊城市或意大利、西西里的希腊移民城市。例如,《一坛金子》(Aulularia)的故事就发生在雅典某街道;[3]《俘虏》(The Captives)发生在希腊西部埃托利亚(Aetolia)某城市;[4]《两个米内克穆斯》场景设置在希腊西部埃皮丹努斯城(Epidamnus)的一条街道上;[5]《关于驴子》(Asinaria)发生在雅典的一条街道上。[6]由此可见,将场景设置在希腊的罗马戏剧不在少数。

综上所述,希腊文字丰富了罗马人的语言,使之更为多元化。希腊神话是罗马戏剧素材之源泉,为罗马作家带来无限灵感。希腊地区作为戏剧场景,备受

---

[1] 〔古罗马〕普劳图斯等:《古罗马戏剧选》,杨宪益、杨周翰、王焕生译,北京:人民文学出版社,1991,第172页。

[2] 同上。

[3] Plautus, *Plautus* Ⅰ, Loeb Classical Library, Harvard University Press, first published 1916, p. 237.

[4] Plautus, *Plautus* Ⅰ, p. 463.

[5] Plautus, *Plautus* Ⅱ, Loeb Classical Library, Harvard University Press, first printed 1917, p. 367.

[6] Plautus, *Plautus* Ⅰ, p. 127.

罗马作家的青睐。希腊文化在罗马戏剧发展史上留下了深深的烙印。在古罗马早期戏剧中，希腊文化元素俯拾即是。这一方面反映了罗马早期戏剧发展滞后的客观事实，另一方面也说明了罗马文化具有开放性。希腊文化的影响促进了罗马戏剧的繁荣。而有选择地吸纳地中海地区的优秀文化，更为罗马戏剧本土特色的彰显奠定了基础。

参考资料

[1] *Remains of Old Latin* Ⅱ (*Livius*, *Naevius*, *Pacuvius*, *Accius*), Loeb Classical Library, Cambridge, Massachusetts: Harvard University Press, first printed 1936.

[2] 〔古希腊〕埃斯库罗斯等:《古希腊悲剧喜剧全集》，张竹明、王焕生译，南京:译林出版社，2007。

[3] 王焕生:《古罗马文学史》，北京:人民文学出版社，2006。

[4] O. Szemerényi, "The Origins of Roman Drama and

Greek Tragedy", *Hermes*, Vol. 103, No. 3 (1975).

[5] Edna M. Hooker, *Changing Fashions in Ancient Drama* Ⅱ, *Greece & Rome*, Second Series, Vol. 7, No. 2 (Oct., 1960), published by Cambridge University Press on behalf of The Classical Association.

[6] Appian, *Roman History*, Loeb Classical Library, Cambridge, Massachusetts: Harvard University Press, first printed 1912.

[7] R. H. 巴洛:《罗马人》,黄韬译,上海:上海人民出版社,2000。

[8] 〔古罗马〕普劳图斯等:《古罗马戏剧选》,杨宪益、杨周翰、王焕生译,北京:人民文学出版社,1991。

[9] Plautus, *Plautus* Ⅰ, Loeb Classical Library, Cambridge, Massachusetts: Harvard University Press, first published 1916.

[10] Plautus, *Plautus* Ⅱ, Loeb Classical Library, Cambridge, Massachusetts: Harvard University Press, first printed 1917.

二、罗马早期戏剧的本土化

罗马文化随着罗马共和国实力的发展,在希腊文化的影响下,取得了巨大进步。而罗马文化究竟是如何发展成熟的,一直是国内外学界高度关注的问题。本文试图以罗马早期戏剧为切入点,追踪罗马戏剧在引入希腊文化后的发展脚步,考察罗马接纳并吸收先进文化的方式。

戏剧是古罗马文学的重要组成部分。古罗马戏剧的繁荣,在很大程度上得益于对希腊文化的继承。早在引入希腊文化之前,罗马本土戏剧已经萌芽,但并未受到重视,直至李维乌斯出现,其历史才翻开了新的一页。李维乌斯将希腊戏剧的清泉引入罗马,并将罗马戏剧带入艺术殿堂。此后,罗马文学史上出现了一批优秀的剧作家,他们为罗马早期戏剧的发展做出了不懈的努力。

二、罗马早期戏剧的本土化

（一）创新剧本内容

古罗马早期剧作家在引入希腊戏剧后，对戏剧的情节加以调整。此时的罗马戏剧作品虽依然充满了希腊戏剧的影子，但其创新性已崭露头角。

在古罗马早期戏剧中，阿克齐乌斯的《关于兵器的判决》(*Armorum Iudicium*)模仿了索福克勒斯的《埃阿斯》(*Αἴας*)。[1]但经过对比可以看到二者的情节设置有所不同。《埃阿斯》的情节从埃阿斯开始疯狂展开，而《关于兵器的判决》所讲述的故事，很明显是从为争夺兵器而举行的比赛开始的。另外，阿克齐乌斯的《阿尔克斯提斯》(*Alcestis*)与欧里庇得斯的《阿尔克斯提斯》(*Ἄλκηστις*)情节十分相似。二者都讲述了阿尔克斯提斯为夫替死，后被赫拉克勒斯救活的故事，但是它们在内容编排上存在着不同之处。在阿克齐乌斯的《阿尔克斯提斯》中，送信人在通报赫拉克勒斯救

---

[1] *Remains of Old Latin* II (*Livius*, *Naevius*, *Pacuvius*, *Accius*), Loeb Classical Library, Cambridge, Massachusetts: Harvard University Press, first printed 1936, p. 358.

了阿尔克斯提斯时说:"当她重新被从地狱带走而尖叫时……"[1]这反映了阿克齐乌斯对赫拉克勒斯如何救回阿尔克斯提斯进行了详细的描述。而欧里庇得斯的《阿尔克斯提斯》只是说赫拉克勒斯要前去将那女子救回,没有描写具体的过程,并在新的一场开篇便讲他已经将她救回了。[2]而且希腊作品中也没有送信人这个角色。这说明阿克齐乌斯调动了自己的想象力,在希腊作品的基础上添加了新内容,并通过增加角色来将此内容展示给读者和观众。

帕库维乌斯的《彭透斯》(Pentheus)与欧里庇得斯的《酒神的伴侣》(βάκχαι)情节十分相似,但亦有不同。在帕库维乌斯的作品中,彭透斯所抓的不是酒神本尊,而是他的一个追随者阿考伊特丝(Acoetes)。[3]此外,在《彭透斯》中有这样的描述:"彭透斯在吩咐要对他加倍处罚后,命令将他加上镣铐关进大牢。但是当监狱的大门自动地打开,阿考伊特丝的镣铐也从

---

[1] *Remains of Old Latin* II (*Livius*, *Naevius*, *Pacuvius*, *Accius*), p. 333.
[2] 〔古希腊〕埃斯库罗斯等:《古希腊悲剧喜剧全集》第5卷,张竹明、王焕生译,南京:译林出版社,2007,第439—448页。
[3] *Remains of Old Latin* II (*Livius*, *Naevius*, *Pacuvius*, *Accius*), p. 275.

其身上脱落时,彭透斯十分地吃惊。"[1] 而在希腊剧本中,彭透斯则要求"把他关进附近的马厩"。[2] 而且狄俄尼索斯说:"我这是耍了他一下:他以为把我绑起来了,其实连碰都没碰着,更不用说绑了,虽然他希望如此。他在把我带去关押的那个牲口棚里,发现了一头牛,用铁链捆了它的腿和脚,怒气冲冲浑身冒汗。"[3]

我们可以通过表格更加清晰地看到二者的区别:

表1 帕库维乌斯的《彭透斯》与欧里庇得斯的
《酒神的伴侣》对比表

罗马	希腊
《彭透斯》 帕库维乌斯 著	《酒神的伴侣》 欧里庇得斯 著
彭透斯在吩咐要对他加倍处罚后,命令将他加上镣铐关进大牢。	彭透斯要求"把他关进附近的马厩"。
但是当监狱的大门自动地打开,阿考伊特丝的镣铐也从其身上脱落时,彭透斯十分地吃惊。	狄俄尼索斯:"我这是耍了他一下:他以为把我绑起来了,其实连碰都没碰着,更不用说绑了,虽然他希望如此。他在把我带去关押的那个牲口棚里,发现了一头牛,用铁链捆了它的腿和脚,怒气冲冲浑身冒汗。"

情节调整后的罗马戏剧不仅继承了希腊作品的精

---

[1] *Remains of Old Latin* Ⅱ (*Livius*, *Naevius*, *Pacuvius*, *Accius*), p. 275.
[2] 〔古希腊〕埃斯库罗斯等:《古希腊悲剧喜剧全集》第5卷,第243页。
[3] 〔古希腊〕埃斯库罗斯等:《古希腊悲剧喜剧全集》第5卷,第249页。

华，还加入了罗马剧作家自己的想象，这是罗马早期戏剧本土化的开端。改编后的罗马戏剧受到了观众的欢迎，丰富了罗马人的文化生活。

（二）探索新发展道路

随着罗马戏剧的发展，剧作家们逐渐摆脱希腊戏剧的束缚，不仅在模仿时加入罗马本土文化和思想，还逐渐开辟出新的发展道路，开始选取一些拉丁题材进行创作，并且在场景选择上也更多地倾向于意大利地区。

第一,在罗马戏剧中,神灵的地位发生了变化。神，不再像在希腊戏剧中那样只是希腊人的神，而是所有凡人的神。在阿克齐乌斯的《酒神的信徒》(Bacchae)里，特瑞西阿斯赞美狄俄尼索斯时说："因为没有人能够创造或拥有足够的言辞来表达他的伟大。"[1] 而在欧里庇得斯的悲剧《酒神的伴侣》中，特瑞西阿斯则说："你所讥笑的这位新神，我没法说出，他在希腊将有

---

[1] *Remains of Old Latin* Ⅱ (*Livius*, *Naevius*, *Pacuvius*, *Accius*), p. 397.

多么伟大。"[1] 显然，此处阿克齐乌斯有意将"希腊"这个限定去掉了，因为这时的狄俄尼索斯已经与罗马的酒神形象融合了。与崇尚小国寡民的希腊不同，罗马当时是一个走出意大利半岛，走向地中海，面向世界的大帝国。罗马人眼中的世界显然不同于希腊人眼中的世界。因此罗马的神也就不会像希腊的神那样仅管辖希腊地区，而是影响整个世界。

敬神是罗马人所推崇的重要美德之一。罗马人眼中的神，不同于希腊人眼中的神。希腊人的神是人性化的神，兼具美德和缺点，拥有和人一样的欲望。但严肃的罗马人眼中的神，拥有绝对尊严，是必须严格服从的。[2] 在阿克齐乌斯的《酒神的信徒》中，特瑞西阿斯告诉卡德摩斯年龄不是拒绝神灵的借口时说："因为不管是衰老、死亡，还是威严的长辈都不。"[3] 而在欧里庇得斯的《酒神的伴侣》中，特瑞西阿斯说："其实这位神并没有划出界限，规定只许年轻人或只许老年人参加舞蹈，他希望人人都崇拜他，并不想把哪部

---

[1] 〔古希腊〕埃斯库罗斯等：《古希腊悲剧喜剧全集》第5卷，第228页。

[2] 此处受到北京师范大学历史学院杨共乐教授的启发。

[3] *Remains of Old Latin* II（*Livius*，*Naevius*，*Pacuvius*，*Accius*），p. 397.

分人排除在外,不让崇拜。"[1] 同样是说老年人也应该崇拜酒神,但是流露出的感觉不一样。罗马作品中表达的意思更为严格,即"老年"不是不崇拜的借口。进一步讲就是说对神的崇拜是必须的,没有理由也要这样做,更没有理由不这样做。而希腊版本则表示人应该崇拜神,因为它猜想神是希望所有人都崇拜他的,也就是说对神崇拜是有原因的,即神没有规定什么人可以参加崇拜他的仪式,并且希望人们都来崇拜他。前者表达了罗马人认为对神的崇拜是没有理由且必须的,后者说明了应该崇拜的理由。由此我们可以感受到希腊作品语气相对缓和些。因为一个人在没有理由的情况下必须做一件事,就是一种根深蒂固的、不可推翻的信念。相反,任何理由都存在着被推翻的可能性,那么倘若做某事是有理由作为前提的,那么做此事的必要性就有可能被推翻。因此,通过这两段文字的对比,我们可以看到罗马人在戏剧中表现出的对神的敬畏。这与在希腊戏剧中,作家任意挥洒神的人性化的一面截然不同。

---

[1] 〔古希腊〕埃斯库罗斯等:《古希腊悲剧喜剧全集》第5卷,第225页。

二、罗马早期戏剧的本土化

第二，罗马戏剧取材日益本土化。李维乌斯是古罗马第一位诗人，也是第一位将希腊戏剧引入罗马的作家。他原是一个希腊人，公元前272年被作为年轻的奴隶带往罗马。[1] 从其目前流传下来的戏剧残篇来看，李维乌斯的悲剧作品全部取材于希腊神话。但继李维乌斯之后的各位剧作家们，都或多或少地创作了一些以罗马本土文化为素材的戏剧作品。在这方面，奈维乌斯留给我们的有《克拉斯提狄乌姆》(*Clastidium*)和《罗穆路斯》(或《狼》)。《克拉斯提狄乌姆》根据罗马人战胜山南高卢的战争改编而成。这场战争的领导者是执政官M.克劳迪乌斯·马赛鲁斯（M. Claudius Marcellus）和Cn.科尼利乌斯·西庇阿（Cn. Cornelius Scipio）。[2] 剧作家帕库维乌斯的《保卢斯》(*Paulus*)也是取材于罗马本土，讲述的是公元前168年执政官卢奇乌斯·埃米利乌斯·保卢斯（Lucius Aemilius Paulus）在皮得那（Pydna）战胜马其顿国王珀尔修斯（Perseus）的故事。[3] 阿克齐乌斯的《埃涅阿斯

---

[1] *Remains of Old Latin* II (*Livius*, *Naevius*, *Pacuvius*, *Accius*), p. ix.

[2] *Remains of Old Latin* II (*Livius*, *Naevius*, *Pacuvius*, *Accius*), p. 137.

[3] *Remains of Old Latin* II (*Livius*, *Naevius*, *Pacuvius*, *Accius*), p. 302.

之子》(*Aeneadae*)[或《德齐乌斯》(*Decius*)]和《布鲁图斯》(*Brutus*)也是拉丁历史剧。《埃涅阿斯之子》讲的是公元前295年,德西乌斯·穆斯(Decius Mus)在攻打萨莫奈人和高卢人的森提乌姆战役中,效仿其父,牺牲自己的事情。[1]《布鲁图斯》则展现了促使罗马人推翻王政、建立共和国的历史事件。[2]这些戏剧内容都已不再是重复希腊的神话传说,而是取材于本土,讲述罗马人自己的故事,传递罗马人自己的精神。

第三,罗马戏剧场景越来越多地设置在罗马地区。例如,"为了使自己的以希腊社会生活为背景的喜剧和罗马社会现实联系得更加紧密,普劳图斯常常在剧中加进罗马生活细节,包括对罗马现实生活现象的描写和罗马政治、法律、宗教观念的引用等,结果变成剧中故事虽然仍然发生在希腊……但剧中人物(希腊人)却往往受罗马官员管辖,遵循罗马法律,呼吁罗马神明,信守罗马宗教观念,活动于罗马广场式的

---

[1] *Remains of Old Latin* Ⅱ(*Livius*, *Naevius*, *Pacuvius*, *Accius*), p. 553.
[2] *Remains of Old Latin* Ⅱ(*Livius*, *Naevius*, *Pacuvius*, *Accius*), pp. 560–561.

二、罗马早期戏剧的本土化

政治、集市中心"[1]。不仅如此,普劳图斯喜剧的故事背景也已经开始逐步走出希腊了。他在《孪生兄弟》[即《两个米内克穆斯》(*Menaechmi*)]的开场词中说:"诗人们在喜剧中常常这样安排:他们把所描写的事情全都设想发生在希腊……而我则声明:我决不这样做,故事发生在哪里,就说在哪里。诚然,此剧的情节也是希腊式的,不过不是阿提卡式的,而是西西里式的。"[2]这说明普劳图斯的戏剧背景不再拘泥于希腊。而另一位戏剧家奈维乌斯则将喜剧《预言者》(*Ariolus*)的场景明确设置在意大利,并在作品中提到了"意大利人"[3]。

我们看到,剧作家们不再简单地翻译和模仿希腊戏剧,或单纯地从希腊神话中汲取灵感,也不再将场景拘泥于希腊地区,而是转向罗马本土文化,将罗马民族的历史故事和对神的敬仰融入戏剧创作当中,充分利用自己的智慧,创作出了匠心独运、特点突出的

---

[1] 〔古罗马〕普劳图斯等:《古罗马戏剧选》,杨宪益、杨周翰、王焕生译,北京:人民文学出版社,1991,译本序,第6页。
[2] 〔古罗马〕普劳图斯等:《古罗马戏剧选》,第172页。
[3] *Remains of Old Latin* II (*Livius*, *Naevius*, *Pacuvius*, *Accius*), p. 81.

新的戏剧作品。

(三)推进理论发展

随着罗马文化的不断发展,罗马戏剧不仅在创作实践上成果显著,而且在理论建设上也取得了很大的进步。开始有人明确提出不应简单地翻译希腊戏剧,此人就是卢基利乌斯(Lucilius)。卢基利乌斯是同时代作家中的佼佼者,他的作品受希腊戏剧影响极小。卢基利乌斯对很多著名的剧作家都进行过讽刺,对其同时代的作家则批评得更为严厉。[1] 卢基利乌斯反对在作品中过多地使用希腊语,认为罗马人不应该让希腊文代替美妙的拉丁语,并且毫不留情地讽刺罗马作家过多地模仿希腊戏剧。在其《讽刺作品》的第二十九卷中,有一部分内容专门用来进行戏剧批评。在这部分内容里,卢基利乌斯就曾通过诙谐地模仿帕库维乌斯的《克律塞斯》(*Chryses*)来对其加以讽刺。[2]

---

[1] *Remains of Old Latin* III (*Lucilius*), Loeb Classical Library, Cambridge, Massachusetts: Harvard University Press, first published 1938, p. xvi.

[2] *Remains of Old Latin* III (*Lucilius*), p. 215.

二、罗马早期戏剧的本土化

由于古罗马早期戏剧作品的不断增加，作家创作及演出经验逐渐丰富，一些剧作家开始着手总结戏剧创作和舞台表演方面的经验，并就文字的使用制定了一系列规则，推动了拉丁文法的进步。在这方面做出贡献的首推阿克齐乌斯。他的《（戏剧写作）要领》（*Pragmatica*）讨论了适合于舞台表演的不同种类的文体和语言。[1] 在该作品残篇中，阿克齐乌斯提到："……在舞台上表演，品味不是很高的普通民众。"还有，"由于这一点，诗人们受到了责骂，更多地是源于你们的头脑太过轻信和庸俗，而非他们的错误"[2]。这显然是在讨论喜剧作家的职责，以及观众们的不足。此外，阿克齐乌斯的《（舞台）指导书》（*Didascalicon Libri*）按照年代顺序梳理了各位剧作家及其作品，并对著名的演员予以特别说明。这部作品至少分为九卷，内容涉及希腊和罗马的舞台剧的各种问题。[3] 例如，阿克齐乌斯认为欧里庇得斯将合唱队同表演分割开来是错误的："……但是欧里庇得斯的，他将合唱队放入他的戏

---

[1] *Remains of Old Latin* II (*Livius, Naevius, Pacuvius, Accius*), p. 589.

[2] *Remains of Old Latin* II (*Livius, Naevius, Pacuvius, Accius*), p. 589

[3] *Remains of Old Latin* II (*Livius, Naevius, Pacuvius, Accius*), p. 578.

剧的方式实在是有欠妥当……"并且讨论了舞台设置以及演员的服装、道具："……演员们的袖子、肩带以及剑。"[1] 阿克齐乌斯是第一个尝试使用拉丁语进行此类总结的人。他的《(舞台)指导书》模仿的是希腊作品《舞台指导》(*Χορὸν Διδασκαλίαι*)，但涵盖的内容更为广泛，反映出在戏剧理论方面，罗马剧作家在吸收希腊成果的基础上，有了进一步的发展，提出了自己的观点，开辟了新的理论空间。

在戏剧的文字使用方面，阿克齐乌斯还提倡在写作悲剧或其他作品时使用拉丁文，并制定了一些拉丁文的文法规则。例如，他要求在写作的时候，对于元音的长短应有所区分，为了表示长元音 ā、ē 和 ū，应双写元音字母（即 aa、ee、uu），同时长元音 ī 应写作 ei；至于软腭音 n 跟一个腭音的情况，也应有特定的表达方式，即 ng 应用 gg 来表示，nc 用 gc 表示。因此，阿克齐乌斯用 "aggueis" 表示 "aguis"、"aggulus" 表示 "angulus"（希腊文写法为 ἄγγυις、ἄγγυλος）。他还提出在字母 a 前应用 k 代替 c，在字母 u 前用 q 代替 c。

---

[1] *Remains of Old Latin* II (*Livius*, *Naevius*, *Pacuvius*, *Accius*), p. 583.

二、罗马早期戏剧的本土化

值得注意的是,阿克齐乌斯反对在拉丁文中使用字母y和z,并且主张在写作过程中应严格保留希腊名词和名字的拼写。他也身体力行,在自己作品中遵从这两项规则。例如,他一直都把"scaena"一字写为"scena",因为其希腊文是σκηνή。[1] 他会提出这样的要求,原因在于字母y实际上是来自希腊语的第二十个字母upsilon(u),而z也是共和后期为拼写源于希腊文的单词而增加的。阿克齐乌斯这样做,并非抵制使用希腊语,而是反对罗马人随意混用拉丁、希腊两种语言,任意将希腊文字融入拉丁文中。这反映出阿克齐乌斯对学习希腊文化的态度比较保守,接纳的同时还有所保留,既不希望破坏希腊语原有的规则,也不愿看到拉丁文失去原有的纯正。阿克齐乌斯制定的这些文法,得到了罗马人民的重视,并在罗马文化的后续发展中产生了深远影响。

罗马早期戏剧创作实践的发展带动了理论的进步。戏剧批评的出现,舞台经验的总结,以及对拉丁文法的规范,都是罗马早期戏剧走向成熟的表现。不

---

[1] *Remains of Old Latin* Ⅱ (*Livius*, *Naevius*, *Pacuvius*, *Accius*), pp. xxii–xxiii.

管是卢基利乌斯在戏剧内容上追求的本土化，还是阿克齐乌斯在理论上的创新和提升，都说明了罗马戏剧已成功转型，不再囿于模仿希腊戏剧，而是走出了一条具有罗马特色的创作之路。

（四）结语

古罗马早期戏剧的发展历程，犹如园艺业中的嫁接技艺，即在罗马文化的"砧木"上嫁接上希腊戏剧的"接穗"，最终产生的果实兼具双方优点，且更富活力。罗马早期戏剧大致经历了简单模仿、逐步修改、自主创新三个阶段。古罗马戏剧发端之时具有浓厚的希腊文化色彩，本土特色并不明显。这在很大程度上是因为罗马最早的剧作家是希腊人，对拉丁文化了解不多，拉丁语水平也不高。随着罗马戏剧的发展，越来越多的罗马本土作家开始出现。罗马文化元素在戏剧中所占比重明显增加，逐渐与希腊文化旗鼓相当。最后，古罗马戏剧步入正轨，优秀剧作不断涌现，剧中的本土化元素超越了希腊元素。剧作家开始抛开希腊剧本和神话，以罗马本土故事为素材进行创作。在写作实践进步的同时,他们在理论研究上也有了新的突破。

总体而言,古罗马戏剧的发展经历了一个本土化的过程。这说明罗马人是一个善于学习和模仿的民族。他们对其他文化的吸纳并非简单地套用,而是结合本民族特色将其本土化,使之适应罗马人民自身的需求。所以,罗马人对其他民族文化的模仿只是外形上的模仿。在内涵方面,他们拥自己的特色。

罗马戏剧的本土化过程,体现了拉丁民族的价值观和罗马文化的发展特点,即对外来文化兼具保守和包容的态度。罗马人具有自己的个性和喜好,对希腊文化也是批判性地吸收,以包容的姿态欢迎希腊文化的引入,又以保守的态度抵制它的全面渗透;在对异族文明给予尊重的同时,也流露出对本土文化的热爱之情和保护之意。

参考资料

[1] *Remains of Old Latin* Ⅱ (*Livius*, *Naevius*, *Pacuvius*, *Accius*), Loeb Classical Library,

Cambridge, Massachusetts: Harvard University Press, first printed 1936.
[2]〔古希腊〕埃斯库罗斯等:《古希腊悲剧喜剧全集》第5卷,张竹明、王焕生译,南京:译林出版社,2007。
[3]〔古希腊〕荷马:《奥德修记》,杨宪益译,上海:上海译文出版社,1979。
[4] 王焕生:《古罗马文学史》,北京:人民文学出版社,2006。
[5]〔古罗马〕普劳图斯等:《古罗马戏剧选》,杨宪益、杨周翰、王焕生译,北京:人民文学出版社,1991。
[6] *Remains of Old Latin* Ⅲ (*Lucilius*), Loeb Classical Library, Cambridge, Massachusetts: Harvard University Press, first published 1938.
[7] 杨共乐:《早期罗马宗教传统的特点》,载《河北学刊》,2008年02期。

三、历史学对修辞学的偏见

在 20 世纪末 21 世纪初,越来越多的学者开始重视史学作品当中的修辞学因素。比勒费尔德(Bielefeld)大学的学者约昂·吕森(Jörn Rüsen)在其论文《历史学的修辞与美学:利奥波德·冯·兰克》中说:"最近史学理论倾向于强调历史编纂学当中的诗歌性和修辞性特点——也正是那些在大多数专业史家的自我认知和自我理解过程中通常被忽略的特点。"[1] 安东尼·伊斯特霍普(Antony Easthope)的文章《渲染文字

---

[1] Jörn Rüsen, "Rhetoric and Aesthetics of History: Leopold von Ranke", *History and Theory*, Vol. 29, No. 2, p.190: "In remarkable opposition to this opinion, recent trends in the theory of history stress the poetical and rhetorical character of historiography—precisely the character generally overlooked in the self-awareness and self-understanding of most professional historians."

意图：历史写作与修辞学》[1]，全面而深入地探讨了历史研究到底在什么程度和角度上是对修辞学的运用，在什么程度和角度上是对独立于"叙述"的事实的描述。安·瑞格尼（Ann Rigney）的《历史学表述中的修辞学》[2]一书则通过修辞学分析，对三部叙述法国大革命历史的史学作品进行研究，探究了史学写作如何建构现实，挑战现实，并且受到现实的约束，指出语言和客观现实不可能完全相同，但历史学表述中的修辞不会创造一个新世界；史家可以自由选择叙述的方式，却绝不能任意创造世界。[3] 罗纳德·卡彭特（Ronald Carpenter）在《作为修辞学的历史：风格、叙述和说

---

[1] Antony Easthope, "Romancing the Stone: History-Writing and Rhetoric", *Social History*, Vol. 18, No. 2.（将"Stone"译为"文字意图"是因为安东尼·伊斯特霍普在其文章中对"Stone"的含义作出如下表述："Although I shall refer for convenience to 'Stone' I shall mean by this not an author and a person but the intention of the words of the text as they may be constructed."）

[2] Ann Rigney, *The Rhetoric of Historical Representation: Three Narrative Histories of the French Revolution*, Cambridge, England: Cambridge University Press, 1990.

[3] Lloyd S. Kramer, "*The Rhetoric of Historical Representation: Three Narrative Histories of the French Revolution* by Ann Rigney", *History and Theory*, Vol. 31, No. 3（Oct., 1992）.

三、历史学对修辞学的偏见

服》[1]这本书中,利用科学的史学和传统的文学分析方法,论证了史学的修辞学性,主张"历史学"能够利用修辞学的资源,塑造公众对世界的认识。[2]与此同时,国内学者也越发关注修辞对于史学作品的意义。福建师范大学刘亚猛教授在其著作《西方修辞学史》[3]绪论中,总结了20世纪60年代以后西方学者对"历史修辞"的态度。复旦大学周兵教授的论文《西方古典修辞学与史学——以修昔底德为例》[4],通过分析修昔底德的《伯罗奔尼撒战争史》,考察了古典修辞学对史学的影响。此外,还有学者翻译引进了西方学者的相关研究。例如,斯特拉斯堡大学教授保罗·里科尔的探讨史学与修辞学关系的文章《历史学和修辞学》[5]就被译成了

---

[1] Ronald H. Carpenter, *History as Rhetoric: Style, Narrative, and Persuasion*. Columbia, SC: University of South Carolina Press, 1995.

[2] S. Michael Halloran, "*History as Rhetoric: Style, Narrative, and Persuasion* by Ronald H. Carpenter", *Rhetorica: A Journal of the History of Rhetoric*, Vol. 15, No. 3.

[3] 刘亚猛:《西方修辞学史》,北京:外语教学与研究出版社,2008。

[4] 周兵:《西方古典修辞学与史学——以修昔底德为例》,载《史学理论研究》,2004,第3期。

[5] 〔法〕保罗·里科尔:《历史学和修辞学》,元熙译,载《第欧根尼》,1996,第1期。

中文。2005年复旦大学第二届修辞学沙龙,专门以修辞学与史学的关系为核心论题,探讨了历史学当如何接受修辞,修辞学又该如何回应历史学,并在学科对话中谋求发展的问题。

这些成果都反映了修辞学对历史学的重要意义。它是史学作品表述的工具,承载着史家求真之理想,同时又威胁着史作的客观性。然而,如此关键的因素,又为何如约昂·吕森所言,"在大多数专业史家的自我认知和自我理解过程中通常被忽略"?事实上,这种"忽略"是有其原因的。回顾史学发展的历程,可以看到"历史学"作为一门学科,在20世纪90年代以前,[1] 其自我认知的过程就是一个竭力摆脱修辞学干扰的过程。

西方修辞学,"传统上一直被等同于'言说的艺术'(the art of speaking)或者'说服的艺术'(the art of persuasion)"。[2] 既然以令受众"心服"为目标,修辞学者始终致力于提高修辞作品的"说服力"。修辞学也在这种追求中不断完善。"公元前470年左右,修辞学

---

[1] 即后—后现代历史哲学出现之前。
[2] 刘亚猛:《西方修辞学史》,绪论,第1页。

三、历史学对修辞学的偏见

的一些基本原则和规范已经逐步确立起来,其中包括选题(invention)、布局(arrangement)和风格(style)等要素。"[1] 这三个要素可以与同样具有文学性的史学文本的三个制作阶段——探究、编纂、成文,形成对应。"探究"是西方史学工作的基本特征。学者在探究的过程中,搜集史料,记录历史的真相,思考历史事件的原因。探究的结果就是史家的论题,因此探究的过程也就是选题的过程。演说术的布局与历史学的编纂同样都是在进行文章结构的组织安排。而"风格"所包括的两个方面——遣词和造句,也是史学作品在成文过程中不可或缺的工作。这样的"对应关系",带来的就是"三要素"对"三阶段"的"对应影响"。而西方史学在自我认知过程中,对修辞学的排斥,也均存在于这三个阶段当中。

在西方,史家对史学自身的理论和历史具有自觉意识的标志,是公元 2 世纪罗马帝国学者琉善[2] 所作

---

[1] 周兵:《西方古典修辞学与史学——以修昔底德为例》,第 57 页。

[2] 琉善的生卒年不详,很可能出生于公元 115—125 年左右,去世于 180 年前后,也就是说他生活在图拉真晚期,经过哈德良和两安敦尼统治阶段,很有可能活到了康茂德担任元首的时候,是当时帝国的一位重要学者。琉善的名字源自拉丁语"Lucius"。他经常用希腊

的《论撰史》。[1]这部在西方史学史上占据重要地位的史学理论作品,批判了当时一些错误的写史方法。这些批判,从"内容"的角度看,可以划归到史学文本制作的三个阶段中;而若从"对象"的角度考察,则主要是针对修辞学在这三阶段中对历史写作的干扰。

第一,从选题阶段开始,就有很多所谓的"历史学者",由于滥用修辞学而受到琉善犀利的讽刺。琉善批评当时很多史家并不知道如何选题,以为想到什么就写什么便可。他指出拙劣的史家最容易犯的一类

语拼法将之写成 "Lycinos"。琉善作品众多,内容深刻,所涉学科范围很广。克鲁瓦塞认为:琉善是希腊天才几乎不再具有创新性的时期出现的唯一具有独创思想的思想家。(Alfred Croiset, Maurice Croiset, *An Abridged History of Greek Literature*, translated by George F. Heffelbower, A. M., London: Macmillan Company, 1904, p. 542.)"这一时期我们能够遇到的唯一伟大的名字就是琉善。"(Alfred Croiset, Maurice Croiset, *An Abridged History of Greek Literature*, p. 519.)科瓦略夫在其著作《古代罗马史》中将琉善和普鲁塔克并称为当时"两位具有世界声名的作家",并称赞他终于能够克服"'诡辩术'并成为古典时期的最后一位伟大的讽刺作家"。([俄]科瓦略夫:《古代罗马史》,王以铸译,上海:上海书店出版社,2007,第736页,第737页)恩格斯则更将琉善比作"古希腊罗马时代的伏尔泰"。([德]恩格斯:《论早期基督教的历史》,见《马克思恩格斯全集(第22卷)》,北京:人民出版社,1965,第527页)

[1] 周文玖:《中国史学史学科的产生和发展》,北京:北京师范大学出版社,2002,第246页。

三、历史学对修辞学的偏见

错误:"他们当中大多数人都忽略了记述事件,而花费大把时间赞美统治者和将军,把自己一方吹捧到天上,而将敌人一方贬低得一文不值。他们不了解历史与颂辞之间的区别和界线不是一条窄窄的地峡,而是一堵宏伟的高墙。"[1] 针对这类问题,琉善认为"路逢侠客须呈剑,不是才人莫献诗":优秀的史著是要给真正有判断力的读者欣赏的,而非为获得庸俗之人的好评。同时,历史作品不是献给当代人的赞词,而是要为后世读者服务。史家在撰写历史的时候,如果选择了错误的评判标准,那么最终他的作品将会变得不伦不类,丧失了历史应有的纯洁和特质。若史家"企图利用史学作品来追求利益,满足一己私欲,其同时代人会厌恶他们,将其视为没有任何能力的露骨的谄媚者,后人则会因为他们的夸张而对整个史学都产生怀疑"[2]。琉善强调历史学的目的在于真实记录,而非献媚于个别人物,那些谄媚的文章不配被称为史作。

琉善将史学作品的受众与修辞学作品的受众区分

---

[1] Lucian, *How to Write History*, 7.

[2] Lucian, *How to Write History*, 13.

开来。在古代,修辞学与演说术的概念有着大量重叠之处;前者主要为后者服务,以最大限度提升语言和文字所要表达的效果。[1]因此,演说术致力于服务当下的受众(主要是"听众")。"言说是使人之所以成为人的一个基本能力,而用说服取代强制与暴力作为协调群体行为的主要手段则是人类文明、人类社会和人类社群形成和发展的一个基本条件。"[2]是故修辞学从诞生之日起便肩负着政治使命——取悦听众,并获得听者支持,因而选题的有益性和有趣性就在修辞学中受到强调。"在言说中,最重要的莫过于赢得听者的好感以及深深地打动听者,使他好像是受一种内心冲动和情感的驱使,而不是根据审思和判断行事。"[3]而琉善认为,史学作品的受众,不应是当代人,而应是未来的读者;[4]不应是作者为眼前利益而取悦、煽动

---

[1] 周兵:《西方古典修辞学与史学——以修昔底德为例》。

[2] 刘亚猛:《西方修辞学史》,绪论,第1页。

[3] 刘亚猛:《西方修辞学史》,第112页。

[4] 琉善在《论撰史》中四次强调,写史不是为当代读者服务的,而是要着眼于未来的读者,分别出现在 Lucian, *How to Write History*, 9, 13, 40, 61。这样从正面直接反复强调的做法,在他的其他文章中并不多见。可见琉善对此观点之重视。

三、历史学对修辞学的偏见

的对象,而应是具有理性和判断力的人。由于受众不同,所以史学作品在选题过程中必须尊重历史的客观性,以保持史学的纯洁。史学家要秉承"求真"的原则,在选题和搜集史料时,保持谨慎的态度和有理性的判断:"史家在搜集史料时不可大意,而是要经过勤勉而艰辛的调查。如果可以的话,他就应该尽量做到亲眼目睹,如若不能,也要选择听取那些更加公正的讲述,聆听那些最不可能因个人喜好或怨恨而对事实进行增减的人。"[1] 由此可见,琉善通过批评个别史学作品中的修辞学特点,对史作读者予以定位,并由此提出了史学作品在选题过程中应秉持的原则,从而对史学应有的品质进行初步认知。

第二,对史家在文章编纂过程中所犯的错误,琉善也提出了批评。有的作家分不清历史和哲学的区别,用推理的方式写史:"他急不可耐地想要卖弄一条极'聪明'的论点,于是在序言的第一句话就给读者们用上了辩证法。……紧接着出现的就是一个三段论,然后又一个三段论。"[2] 琉善指出史著就是史著,不是哲

---

[1] Lucian, *How to Write History*, 47.

[2] Lucian, *How to Write History*, 17.

学论著，是要记录史实，而非以展示逻辑推理为目的。修辞学的主要任务就是"说服"。"说服"的重要手段之一就是"陈述的逻辑性"。修辞者在布局谋篇时，可遵循"修辞原则"，考虑采用"引言、事实陈述、观点区分、证明、批驳、结语"这个"六部结构"，或由"论点、理由、理据、修饰、概述"组成的"五部结构"。[1]若选择"五部结构"，则显然是在强调论证的逻辑性。这种对逻辑性的强调使修辞学作品具有明显的哲学特征。而对历史学而言，作品的逻辑是架构内容的工具，其最终任务是要为清晰而充分地展现客观历史服务。因而某些史学作品对逻辑推理的强调，是对修辞学手法的不当应用。而琉善对此现象的批评，则是对修辞学的排斥。如果修辞学者选择的是"六部结构"，那么"引言"则是一个很重要的环节。"……受众往往从'引言'中听出'名誉''不名誉''可疑'和'猥琐'等四种动机。……如果引言给人以部分名誉部分不名誉的印象，修辞者的动机将显得可疑。如果引言谈到的都是些无关紧要的事情，他的动机将显得猥琐。"[2] 开

---

[1] 刘亚猛：《西方修辞学史》，第94页。
[2] 刘亚猛：《西方修辞学史》，第83页。

三、历史学对修辞学的偏见

篇的策略，影响到整部修辞学作品的效果。然而，在史学作品序言的写作上，琉善指出如果没有特别的需要的话，史家不必写正式的序言，只要"以事代序"，把历史大背景说清楚便可。强调史家的序言与演说家的不同，不必讨好读者，只要求读者做到"注意和虚心"即可。史家可以通过阐述自己所述事件的重要性来吸引读者的注意力，通过清晰顺畅的文字来令读者虚心阅读。达到这两点，序言就起到了其应有的作用。可见在史作编纂上，琉善也明确表示史学不必追求修辞学特色。

第三，很多历史作品的成文过程也存在问题。它们追求华丽辞藻，却言之无物。修辞学主张通过在遣词造句和思想内容两个层面运用"辞格"来让言辞更为多彩，表达更为丰富，以使"言说"达到完美。而"比较""强调""描绘"等是"辞格"的重要手法。[1] 在《论撰史》中，某些作家受到批评，正是因为其过分地"描绘"："由于不善于抓住重要内容，或者不知道该写什么，他们转而将笔墨投入到这种对风景、洞穴的描绘上。"[2] 这些历史作者花大力气细致描绘城市、山

---

[1] 刘亚猛：《西方修辞学史》，第92页。
[2] Lucian, *How to Write History*, 20.

川、田野等种种静态景物,却迟迟不肯切入正题叙述史实。他们实际上就是犯了忽略"历史",沉迷于修辞学的"炫技"的错误。琉善提醒他们历史作品要记录史实,而非为描摹山川景物而生。与此同时,"比较"也是2世纪修辞学的典型手法,如《第二代智术师》中所说:"现在的智术师则是因其大范围使用对立比较的方法而令人注目。"[1] 当时一些历史作品就运用了修辞学中夸张的对比,忘却了历史"求真"的重要性。例如,《论撰史》就提到有的史家为了凸显罗马军队的战斗力,甚至会任意编造死伤人数,以形成鲜明的对比:"在优罗配斯(Europus)之战中,敌方有七万零二百三十六人被消灭,而罗马人则仅有两人阵亡,九人受伤。"[2] 对此,琉善批评他们缺乏对史实应有的尊重,任意夸大叙述的内容。此外,还有史家身为写史之人,却不知"求真"的重要性,为了论证自己的论点,或为了突出写作意图,将大量主观的情感加入其中。这样的作家对于历史应当尊重事实这一原则毫

---

[1] 〔英〕安德森:《第二代智术师——罗马帝国的文化现象》,罗卫平译,北京:华夏出版社,2011,第80页。

[2] Lucian, *How to Write History*, 20.

三、历史学对修辞学的偏见

无意识。针对此类作家,琉善指出史家在语言运用上,不应专注于文字雄辩的力度,而应选择简单易懂、质朴无华的语言,"辞藻可以修饰作品但不能喧宾夺主,不要给人刻意堆砌之感"[1]。在写作文风上,琉善认为写作历史,可以有诗人的风度,但同时必须要有史家的限度。不可像写作诗歌那样,任想象力信马由缰地发挥,否则就会"好像在为坚强、粗犷的运动员穿上紫色裙装,为他装扮上一个漂亮妓女的随身物品,并且在其脸上涂抹彩妆"[2]。也就是说,史家可以适当地激扬文字,但不能忘记史学应有的本分,不可随着灵感的牵引任意挥洒笔墨,沉迷于修辞。

总之,琉善在《论撰史》中批评了某些拙劣的史家写历史作品时任意发挥想象力,粉饰历史的真相,堆砌优美的词汇,或者为凸显论述效果,不惜使用夸张的对比或编造"史实"的手段。通过分析可以看到,琉善这些批判,就是在排斥历史作品中的修辞学手法。对错误写史方法的否定,就是对正确方法的肯定。琉善在批评过程中提出了史家应有的素养,以及正确的

---

[1] Lucian, *How to Write History*, 44.

[2] Lucian, *How to Write History*, 8.

写史方法。他强调历史学的意义在于为后人记录下时间长河当中发生的重大事件,以免后人对自己的历史无知。他总结出史学应该具备的几大特点——求真、实用、平易。琉善说:"历史只有一个任务和目标,那就是实用,而实用只根源于真实。"[1] 有人将历史分为"欣赏的历史"和"实用的历史",琉善表示这种观点是错误的。他认为歌颂不是历史的目的,让人赏玩也不是它的追求。因此历史的价值就在于其真实性。如果一篇史作流于奉承和歌颂,那么它也就丧失了被欣赏的价值。历史作品的本质既是求真,就不应是作者炫耀文采的舞台,其文字要做到简单易懂,朴实无华。作为一名历史学家,必须德才兼备:品德上,他要"无所畏惧,清正不阿,独立自主,是自由表达和真理的朋友"[2];在才华上,他应当有深厚的文化底蕴,并能够在写作过程中做到收放自如,张弛有度。由此可见,琉善对于历史学科的特点,以及史家应有的素养已经有了很深入的认识,初步完成了历史学科的自我认知。而这个认知的过程,同时也是一个摆脱修辞学干扰的过程。

---

[1] Lucian, *How to Write History*, 9.

[2] Lucian, *How to Write History*, 41.

三、历史学对修辞学的偏见

不过,历史学的自我认知并非始于琉善,亦非止于琉善。正如布罗代尔所说:"所有学科都在不断地重新界定自己和检验自己。"[1] 上至修昔底德,下至现代史家,都一直在修改历史学的定义。"在西方史学史上,公元前5世纪的雅典将军、历史学家修昔底德,是客观书写历史的榜样。……被认为'旨在用严格的客观方式来表示历史的进程本身'、'思想深邃、富有修辞而又恪守真实'。"[2] 修昔底德在谈到历史的证据时说:"这比诗人的证据更好些,因为诗人常常夸大他们的主题的重要性;也比散文编年史家的证据更好些,因为他们所关心的不在于说出事情的真相而在于引起听众的兴趣,他们的可靠性是经不起检查的;……如果我们考虑到我们是研究古代历史的话,我们可以要求只用最明显的证据,得到合乎情理的正确结论。"[3] 此外,"修昔底德还轻蔑地提到为在演说比赛中获胜而

---

[1] 〔法〕费尔南·布罗代尔:《论历史》,刘北成、周立红译,北京:北京大学出版社,2008,第13页。

[2] 李隆国:《叙事理论对历史研究的影响——以修昔底德的写作策略为例》,载《河北学刊》,2007,第27卷,第1期,第121页。

[3] 〔古希腊〕修昔底德:《伯罗奔尼撒战争史》,谢德风译,北京:商务印书馆,1960,第一卷,第一章,第17页。

写出的历史，轻蔑地提到为取悦凡夫俗子而扩展为寓言的历史"[1]。古代诗歌和史作多以朗诵方式传达给听众，而修昔底德此处强调史学应具备客观性的同时所批评的刻意"夸大"和"迎合取悦"，很显然也是修辞学惯用的技巧。不可否认，修昔底德在《伯罗奔尼撒战争史》中对修辞学也有所运用，但是在对历史学的本质特征——客观性有意识地进行认知的时候，他也同样表现出了对修辞学的排斥。

西方史学发展史上另一位里程碑式的人物是波吕比奥斯[2]（约公元前200年—前118年）。波吕比奥斯是公元前2世纪罗马世界出现的著名历史学家。汤普森将其称为修昔底德之后最伟大的希腊历史家。[3]波

---

[1]〔意〕克罗齐:《历史学的理论和历史》，田时纲译，北京：中国社会科学出版社，2005，第130页。

[2] 有多种翻译方法：廖学盛先生将其译为"波吕比奥斯"；谢德风先生将其译为"波利比阿"；田时刚先生将其译为"波利比奥斯"；褚新国先生将其译为"波利比乌斯"。由于此人名字的希腊文原文是Πολύβιος，因此廖学盛翻译的方式最准确。本文采用廖先生的译法。波吕比奥斯出生于希腊，在参加希腊人反对罗马的战斗失败后被作为人质带到罗马。波吕比奥斯的作品《历史》再现了罗马征服地中海的过程，探究了罗马成功的原因。

[3]〔美〕J.W. 汤普森：《历史著作史》（上卷·第一分册），谢德风译，北京：商务印书馆，1996，第74页。

三、历史学对修辞学的偏见

吕比奥斯也对历史学的自我认知做出了贡献,并且在总结史学作品应有的特点时也批评了史家对修辞学技巧的滥用。例如,波吕比奥斯曾批评费拉克斯(Phylarchus)在形容曼堤尼亚(Mantineans)人民的苦难时植入过多情绪,辞藻过分华丽:"因急于获得读者的怜悯,唤起他们的同情心,他(即费拉克斯)栩栩如生地描绘了女人们紧紧相拥,撕扯着头发,袒胸露乳,不仅如此,他还描述了男男女女在跟其子女和年迈父母一起被掳走囚禁时的泪水和哀号。费拉克斯在其'历史'中不断重复施加这样的影响,每次都努力在我们眼前再现恐怖的画面。"[1] 波吕比奥斯所批评的这种通过华丽辞藻煽动读者以获取即得效果的做法,是典型的修辞学手法。而在批评费拉克斯的错误

---

[1] Polybius, *The Rise of the Roman Empire*, Penguin Classics, Suffolk: Richard Clay Ltd., first published 1979, p. 168: "In his eagerness to arouse the pity of his readers and enlist their sympathy through his story he introduces graphic scenes of women clinging to one another, tearing their hair and baring their breasts, and in addition he describes the tears and lamentations of men and women accompanied by their children and aged parents as they are led away into captivity. Phylarchus reproduces this kind of effect again and again in his history, striving on each occasion to recreate the horrors before our eyes."

的同时,波吕比奥斯也明确了史学家的职责:"……用吸引眼球的描述吓唬读者不是历史学家的任务……他的首要任务应该是准确记录真实发生过的和说过的内容。"[1]河南大学学者褚新国曾在其论文《波利比乌斯论撰史中的"失真"问题》[2]中指出,波吕比奥斯所批评的史学作品"失真"的其中一个层面,就是很多史作存在"偏重艺术审美而以辞害意"的不良现象。这种现象主要表现为:为当事人随意虚构演说词,渲染并强调情感化处理历史人事,以及巧言令色的戏剧化叙事。波吕比奥斯对历史作品文风的定位是"真实、质朴",将存在上述现象的作品称为"修辞作品或修辞性演说词作品",[3]拒绝承认它们属于历史学。由此可见,波吕比奥斯在对史学进行认知、定义的过程中,同样旗帜鲜明地将修辞学排斥在外。

---

[1] Polybius, *The Rise of the Roman Empire*, Penguin Classics, Suffolk: Richard Clay Ltd., first published 1979, p. 168: "It is not a historian's business to startle his readers with sensational descriptions, ...it is his task first and foremost to record with fidelity what actually happened and was said, however commonplace this may be."

[2] 褚新国:《波利比乌斯论撰史中的"失真"问题》,载《唐都学刊》,2013,第29卷,第1期。

[3] 褚新国:《波利比乌斯论撰史中的"失真"问题》,第99页。

三、历史学对修辞学的偏见

历史学发展到现代已趋成熟，但现代史家在进行自我定位时，依然强调史学的非修辞学性。"从19世纪中叶开始，随着自然科学的高歌猛进，历史学进入了职业化和规范化的进程。在科学发展和实证主义哲学的影响和推动下，历史学家们开始为历史学争取一种科学的地位。"[1] 例如，以兰克为代表的历史学家坚持认为历史学具有科学性。他们主张"历史学的科学性在于通过对历史事实的广泛搜集和审慎考订，'如实直书'，还历史以本来面貌"[2]。在这个历史学进行自我认知的新阶段里，对史学的科学性的强调，伴随着对其文学性的压制。一些学者就因关心历史作品文学性，而非科学性，而遭到批判。[3] 使历史学具有文学性的媒介是修辞学。是修辞学的遣词造句，完成了历史学文本的生成过程。因此，现代史家对史作文学性的否认，就是对其修辞学性的否认。

回顾西方史学史，历史学自我认知的过程始终伴

---

[1] 董立河：《后现代历史哲学及其对传统历史学的挑战》，载《国外社会科学》，2006，第4期，第23页。

[2] 董立河：《后现代主义之后的历史理性与史学实践》，载《历史研究》，2013，第5期，第43页。

[3] 董立河：《后现代历史哲学及其对传统历史学的挑战》。

随着对修辞学的排斥。也就是说，西方史学走向成熟的过程，就是其摆脱修辞学牵绊的过程。很长一段时间以来，对修辞学的否定，是历史学自我定位时的一个重要任务。因此，修辞学之于史学的意义，曾经在很多史家的自我认知过程中都被忽略了。然而，西方现代历史理性对修辞学的明确压制，并没有完成对历史学的最终认知。后现代历史哲学的解构，给传统史学带来了巨大挑战，而这挑战的切入点正是史学家们一直逃避的史学的修辞学性。后现代主义历史哲学的起点是海登·怀特《元历史学：19世纪欧洲的历史想象》一书的出版。在海登·怀特看来，"历史作品是历史学家将一种叙事强加于过去的产物，因而是一种文学制品。历史知识不是根据经验主义的方式获得的，而是由历史学家的美学决定造成的"[1]。后现代主义认为，依靠语言来构筑的史学文本无法保证其自身的客观性。这一看法将历史学等同于文学，否定了史学作品反映客观史实的可能性，进而取消了历史学科存在的合理性。随着后现代主义出现的就是历史学领域的

---

[1] 董立河：《后现代主义之后的历史理性与史学实践》，载《历史研究》，第46页。

三、历史学对修辞学的偏见

"语言学转向"[1]。这种"转向"使学者关注修辞学的意义。面对后现代主义史学的挑战,后-后现代主义学者在捍卫史学客观性的过程中正视了历史学的修辞学性。"历史首先是历史事实,随后是历史认识,最后才是历史语言。语言之所以能与历史联系在一起,完全是因为语言有助于人们认识历史事实。"[2]要使用语言就不可能回避"言说的艺术",即文本的修辞学性。剑桥大学学者理查德·艾文斯(Richard J. Evans)在其著作《捍卫历史》中说:"内容不是风格的派生物:它能用许多不同的风格来精确描述同一个事情",[3]再次论证了修辞无碍于历史学的存在,而且对史学表述具有积极意义。至此,史学的自我认知达到了新的高度。"历史学不同于自然科学,而是立足于求真基础上的人文学科,不能用自然科学的标准来衡量其价值。"[4]

---

[1] 韩震、董立河:《论西方历史哲学的"语言学转向"》,载《北京大学学报》(哲学社会科学版),2005,第42卷,第5期。

[2] 杨共乐:《后现代主义与后现代史学》,载《史学史研究》,2003,第3期,第75页。

[3] 〔英〕理查德·艾文斯:《捍卫历史》,张仲民、潘玮琳、章可译,桂林:广西师范大学出版社,2009,第112页。

[4] 此观点受到北京师范大学历史学院杨共乐教授的启发。

后-后现代主义对"修辞学"的接纳，使历史学者在对待历史文本的问题上找到了平衡点，辩证地看待修辞学对史学作品的意义。于是21世纪初，越来越多的学者开始重视史学作品当中的修辞学因素，在追求历史学文本的客观性的同时，不再回避其文学性，主张合理运用修辞学的叙述和论证手法，更好地帮助历史学实现自我。

参考资料

[1] Jörn Rüsen, "Rhetoric and Aesthetics of History: Leopold von Ranke", *History and Theory*, Vol. 29, No. 2.

[2] Antony Easthope, "Romancing the Stone: History-Writing and Rhetoric", *Social History*, Vol. 18, No. 2.

[3] Ann Rigney, *The Rhetoric of Historical Representation: Three Narrative Histories of the French Revolution*, Cambridge, England: Cambridge University Press, 1990.

[4] Lloyd S. Kramer, "*The Rhetoric of Historical*

Representation: Three Narrative Histories of the French Revolution by Ann Rigney", *History and Theory*, Vol. 31, No. 3 (Oct., 1992).

[5] Ronald H. Carpenter, *History as Rhetoric: Style, Narrative, and Persuasion*. Columbia, SC: University of South Carolina Press, 1995.

[6] S. Michael Halloran, "*History as Rhetoric: Style, Narrative, and Persuasion* by Ronald H. Carpenter", *Rhetorica: A Journal of the History of Rhetoric*, Vol. 15, No. 3.

[7] 刘亚猛:《西方修辞学史》,北京:外语教学与研究出版社,2008。

[8] 周兵:《西方古典修辞学与史学——以修昔底德为例》,载《史学理论研究》,2004,第3期。

[9] 〔法〕保罗·里科尔:《历史学和修辞学》,元熙译,载《第欧根尼》,1996,第1期。

[10] Alfred Croiset, Maurice Croiset, *An Abridged History of Greek Literature*, translated by George F. Heffelbower, A. M., London: Macmillan Company, 1904.

[11]〔俄〕科瓦略夫:《古代罗马史》,王以铸译,上海:上海书店出版社,2007。

[12]〔德〕恩格斯:《论早期基督教的历史》,见《马克思恩格斯全集(第22卷)》,北京:人民出版社,1965。

[13]周文玖:《中国史学史学科的产生和发展》,北京:北京师范大学出版社,2002。

[14] Lucian, *How to Write History*, in Lucian, *Lucian* Ⅵ, Loeb Classical Library, Cambridge, Massachusetts: Harvard University Press, 1959.

[15]〔英〕安德森:《第二代智术师——罗马帝国的文化现象》,罗卫平译,北京:华夏出版社,2011。

[16]〔法〕费尔南·布罗代尔:《论历史》,刘北成、周立红译,北京:北京大学出版社,2008。

[17]李隆国:《叙事理论对历史研究的影响——以修昔底德的写作策略为例》,载《河北学刊》,2007,第27卷,第1期。

[18]〔古希腊〕修昔底德:《伯罗奔尼撒战争史》,谢德风译,北京:商务印书馆,1960。

三、历史学对修辞学的偏见

[19] 〔意〕克罗齐:《历史学的理论和历史》,田时纲译,北京:中国社会科学出版社,2005。

[20] 〔美〕J.W. 汤普森:《历史著作史》(上卷·第一分册),谢德风译,北京:商务印书馆,1996。

[21] Polybius, *The Rise of the Roman Empire*, Penguin Classics, Suffolk : Richard Clay Ltd., first published in 1979.

[22] 褚新国:《波利比乌斯论撰史中的"失真"问题》,载《唐都学刊》,2013,第 29 卷,第 1 期。

[23] 董立河:《后现代历史哲学及其对传统历史学的挑战》,载《国外社会科学》,2006,第 4 期。

[24] 董立河:《后现代主义之后的历史理性与史学实践》,载《历史研究》,2013,第 5 期。

[25] 韩震、董立河:《论西方历史哲学的"语言学转向"》,载《北京大学学报》(哲学社会科学版),2005,第 42 卷,第 5 期。

[26] 杨共乐:《后现代主义与后现代史学》,载《史学史研究》,2003,第 3 期。

[27] 〔英〕理查德·艾文斯:《捍卫历史》,张仲民、潘玮琳、章可译,桂林:广西师范大学出版社,2009。

四、罗马与东汉宗教批判思想之比较
——以琉善、王充为例

(一)思想专制之论争

关于汉代是否存在思想专制的问题,长久以来都是学界争论的热点。有的学者认为,古代中国是大一统的社会,从汉代开始便"罢黜百家,独尊儒术",推行文化专制政策。在这种政策下,知识分子遭到严重的迫害。秉持这一观点的代表学者有吴虞、陈独秀、胡适、曹伯韩、翦伯赞、李维武等。[1] 同时,也存在

---

[1] 吴虞:《儒家主张阶级制度之害》,载《新青年》,1917,第3卷第4号,第3页:"自孔氏诛少正卯,著'侮圣言'、'非圣无法'之厉禁;孟轲继之,辟杨墨,攻异端,自附于圣人之徒;董仲舒对策,以为诸

四、罗马与东汉宗教批判思想之比较

大量学者主张汉代没有思想专制——远的有柳诒徵、徐复观,近的有金春峰、李文东、李之喆、马雪芹、

不在六艺之科、孔子之术者,皆绝其道,勿使并进;韩愈《原道》'人其人,火其书,庐其居'之说昌;于是儒教专制统一,中国学术扫地。"陈独秀:《宪法与孔教》,载《新青年》,1916,第2卷,第3号,第2页:"今效汉武之术,罢黜百家,独尊孔氏,则学术思想之专制,其湮塞人智,为祸之烈,远在政界帝王之上。"欧阳哲生编:《胡适文集》第六卷,北京:北京大学出版社,1998,第610页:"这个建议的文字及与精神都与李斯的焚书议是很相像的。他们的主旨都是要'别黑白而定一尊',都是要统一学术思想。"曹伯韩、章太炎:《大师的国学课2——常识与概论》,南昌:江西教育出版社,2013年1月,第92页:"自孔子成为偶像以来,数千年来,没有人敢公开批驳孔子的议论,只除了王充和明代的李卓吾两人。李卓吾的书曾被人焚烧,王充的书幸或保存,这又可见汉朝虽尊崇六经为官学,民间的学术思想仍然自由。"翦伯赞:《秦汉史》,北京:北京大学出版社,1999,第528—529页:"自从董仲舒的建议批准以后,汉代初叶再生出来的一切文化思想,都要站在儒家学说的法庭之前,遭受审判,判定其生存或宣布其死刑。儒家哲学变成了封建制度之最高的政治原理,就成了衡量文化思想之标准的尺度。一切与这种原理相冲突的古典的学说,即使比儒家学说含有更多的真理,也要从头到尾被摧毁。从这一时代起,孔子便从诸子百家之中超升出来,变成了东方世界之罗马教皇,而儒家哲学也就变成永恒不变的真理,谁要批判儒家哲学,谁就是名教的罪人,文化的叛逆。"李维武:《王充与中国文化》,贵阳:贵州人民出版社,2000,第18—19页:"有汉一代,既是中国古代知识分子积极参与现实政治并在学术上取得诸多成就的时代,也是中国古代知识分子在大一统封建专制政治的高压下发出呻吟、流着血泪的时代。"

保守抑或包容

刘桂生、管怀伦等诸位学者。[1]

---

[1] 柳诒徵:《中国文化史》(上),上海:上海古籍出版社,2001,第352—353页:"世多谓汉武帝绌百家,崇儒学,为束缚思想之主因。……恶得以董仲舒、卫绾之言,遽谓武帝,罢黜百家乎?……武帝以后,学者犹兼治诸子百家之学。……使武帝时禁人攻习异端,则向、歆父子,何必校定诸书乎?"徐复观《两汉思想史》第一卷,上海:华东师范大学出版社,2001,第193页:"纵使此种开明态度,不能直接推其出于董仲舒;但最低限度,刘氏父子及班固等,亦丝毫未因董氏'皆绝其道'的话,而发生误解;更未因此影响到他们对学术的全盘态度。"金春峰:《汉代思想史》,北京:中国社会科学出版社,1987,第201页:"'罢黜百家'并不是禁绝各家的著作和思想,搞新的'焚书坑儒',不过是举贤良方正,俊茂异才,不取'百家',不以'百家'作为统治思想而已。"李文东:《"罢黜百家,独尊儒术"与汉武帝的文化政策》,载《许昌师专学报》,1988,第3期,第79页:"'罢黜百家,独尊儒术'的实质既不是董仲舒《天人三策》中'绝其道','邪辟之说灭息',也不是我们通常所说的禁绝百家,而是罢黜前朝所置的诸子博士官,以后唯设儒家五经博士官,不再设诸子博士。确立了儒家的官学地位。汉武帝实行的是在确立儒学统治思想条件下悉延百端之学的文化政策,而非封建文化专制政策。"李之喆:《是统一,而非专制——重评汉武帝"罢黜百家,独尊儒术"的政策》,载《上海大学学报》,1999,第3期,第83页:"汉武帝的'罢黜百家,独尊儒术'的政策,造成了中国文化统一而非专制的局面。汉武帝为实行这个政策所采取的手段是温和的、合理的,所导致的结果也非思想文化的单一与窒息局面。"马雪芹:《"罢黜百家,独尊儒术"新解》,载《人文杂志》,1999,第5期,第134、136页:"'罢黜百家,独尊儒术'的方针,只是说不为儒家之外的其他学派设立专门博士官,并非要禁止诸子百家的思想学说在社会上的流传";"对武帝这一时期在思想政治方面所做的努力和成就,与其用'罢黜百家,独尊儒术'八个字来概括,倒不如用'尊崇儒术,兼容百家'更为确切恰当些。"刘桂生:《刘桂生学术文化

四、罗马与东汉宗教批判思想之比较

以往的研究多从中国古代文本史料出发，追究文献、文字的含义，在中国古代世界的语境下探讨汉代是否存在思想专制。然而，何谓"专制"？"专制"一词在中国虽古已有之，但其含义与现代的"专制"不同。现代学者所使用的专制的概念来自西方，发源自古代地中海世界。[1] 不仅如此，在任何政治背景下，思想的专制或自由程度，都是一个相对的问题，与其所在的时代的大背景有着密切的关系。既然不能绝对化，就需借助外在标尺加以衡量。那么探讨"思想专

随笔》，北京：中国青年出版社，2000，第9页："'罢黜百家'仅仅是对儒学以外的各家，官方不予以倡导，不给予支持、鼓励，而王公贵戚、民间隐逸，若要爱好研习，尽可以自便，只是不能以之猎取功名富贵。……'独尊儒术'则是以儒家思想作为占统治地位的思想。"管怀伦：《汉武帝"罢黜百家，独尊儒术"确有其事——与孙景坛同志商榷》，载《南京社会科学》，1994，总第64期，第17页："罢黜不是消灭，独尊也是崇尚。"

[1] 张分田：《"专制"问题论纲——关于"重建中国思想史知识体系"的若干思考》，载《天津社会科学》，2011，第3期，第120页："现代政治学的'专制'与中国古代的'专制'不是同一概念，此'专制'非彼'专制'。……古代汉语的'专制'一词多用于描述重臣、权臣的权力地位。"施治生：《"东方专制主义"概念的历史考察》，载《史学理论研究》，1993，第3期，第37页："亚里士多德在书中所用的'δεσποτικος'（专制的）一词是个形容词，这个词汇及其相关的副词'δεσποτικως'，均由名词'δεσποτης'派生而来。古希腊文'δεσποτης'，从词源学来说，原意为：(一)家长;(二)奴隶的主人。"

制",就不应仅关起门来"整理国故",还应跳出传统的界限,在世界古代史的视域下考察古代东方的思想自由空间。

(二)王充与琉善的宗教批判

比较研究(Comparative study)的方法,可以将视角定位在中国之外,从而在很大程度上避免偏颇。比较,是认识事物的重要方法。"历史比较不仅可能精确地、令人信服地确定发展的失误,同时它也可以对历史学家对历史发展失误的错误判断以更大的可靠性加以排除和净化。"[1]横向的共时性(Synchronic)的比较可以反映不同的国家、民族、社会集团等在同一历史时期中的同异,可以说明历史的时代特点。[2]在古代东方和西方,都流传着各自的传统宗教。在基督教兴起之前,繁荣于罗马帝国的是以"奥林匹亚诸神"

---

[1]〔德〕哈特穆特·凯博:《历史比较研究导论》,赵进中译,北京:北京大学出版社,2009,第45页。

[2] 刘家和:《历史的比较研究与世界历史》,载《北京师范大学学报(社会科学版)》,1996,第5期,第46—47页。

四、罗马与东汉宗教批判思想之比较

为核心的传统的希腊罗马宗教。在东汉兴盛的,则是由自商周时期流传下来的巫觋活动与秦汉之际产生的谶纬经学交织而成的中国传统宗教。琉善和王充都是著作等身的作者。王充穷尽毕生精力著下《论衡》。据范晔《后汉书·王充传》载:"《论衡》八十五篇,二十余万言。"[1] 而流传下来的冠以琉善之名的文章也有八十二篇。他们在各自的作品当中,均就其所在社会的宗教活动展开了大量的、深入的探讨。本文欲采用比较研究的方法,通过详细比对王充和琉善作品中对占卜、预言的批判,全面把握他们宗教批判思想之异同,同时结合二者各自的时代背景和个人经历,对照2世纪"理性自由时代"[2] 的罗马,考察中国汉朝文人的思想空间。

王充(公元27年—约97年),东汉杰出的思想家,生于东汉建武三年,卒于永元八年。王充出身于没有权势的庶族地主阶层,曾在京师太学深造,毕业后几

---

[1] 范晔撰,李贤等注:《后汉书》(第六册),北京:中华书局,1965,第1629页。
[2] 〔英〕J. B. 伯里:《思想自由史》,周颖如译,北京:商务印书馆,2012,第10页。

次担任县、郡、州的小官,又由于性格刚直而先后去职,最后"归乡里,屏居教授"[1]。晚年在友人推荐下朝廷派车接他做官,被他称病婉拒。[2] 王充典型的特点是"非圣无法"和"疾虚妄",善以理性的精神和科学的态度剖析中国古代宗教。谢夷吾在向汉章帝举荐他时,曾评价说:"充之天才,非学所加,虽前世孟轲、孙卿,近汉扬雄、刘歆、司马迁,不能过也。"[3] 苏联学者阿·阿·彼得洛夫则赞许王充是唯物主义者、无神论者、迷信和愚昧无知的不共戴天的敌人、真实知识的宣扬者……是中国古代真正的、激进的启蒙思想家。[4]

据《论衡·自纪篇》,王充曾著下《讥俗》《节义》《政务》《论衡》《养性》等书。但流传到今日的只有

---

[1] 范晔撰,李贤等注:《后汉书》(第六册),第1629页。

[2] 王充撰,陈蒲清点校:《论衡》,长沙:岳麓书社,2015,前言第1—2页。

[3] 范晔撰,李贤等注:《后汉书》(第六册),第1630页。

[4] 〔苏〕阿·阿·彼得洛夫:《王充——中国古代的唯物主义者和启蒙思想家》,李时译,北京:科学出版社,1956,第81页。

《论衡》。[1]"今本《论衡》有三十卷本和三十五卷本两种,皆为八十五篇。其中第四十四篇《招致》仅存篇目,无正文,实存八十四篇。"[2]王充著书的特点是从实际出发,针对社会存在的现实问题提出个人思考和解决方案。《自纪》载:"充既疾俗情,作讥俗之书;又悯人君之政,徒欲治人,不得其宜,不晓其务,愁精苦思,不睹所趋,故作政务之书。又伤伪书俗文多不实诚,故为论衡之书。"[3]王充的作品由诸多短小的文章组成,涉及内容广泛。《论衡》基本上贯彻了王充"疾虚妄"的精神,力驳世间流行的虚妄思想。中国古代传统宗教作为这些虚妄思想的重要组成部分,受到了王充的重点关注。

琉善的生卒年不详,很可能出生于公元115年—125年左右,去世于180年前后,也就是说他生活在

---

[1] 有的学者认为今本《论衡》已经包含了另外几本佚失的书,也有学者持不同看法。另外,关于《论衡》当中是否有伪作和佚失篇目,也都存有争议。本文目的不在版本考证,故在此对上述问题不加深究。

[2] 黄中业、陈恩林译注:《论衡选译》,南京:凤凰出版社,2011,前言第3页。

[3] 黄晖:《论衡校释》(四),北京:中华书局,1990,第1194页。

保守抑或包容

图拉真晚期，经过哈德良和两安敦尼统治阶段，可能活到了康茂德担任元首的时候。关于琉善的生平，少有资料记载。对于他的经历，我们主要依据其作品内容加以推断。琉善经过了从学习雕刻，改为投身到法庭辩护者和诡辩家所追求的演说生涯，最后转向从事讽刺文学创作。[1]

琉善一生游历甚广，见识广博。他由于各种日常小事等种种机缘写作其作品。与王充相似，他的作品也是简短的小册子、对话、论文或故事，并非鸿篇巨制，但内容涉及罗马帝国社会生活的诸多方面，对日常生活、市民道德，以及历史学、教育学和美学等方面均有所批判和探讨。讽刺对话在其作品中占有很大比重。对话本是哲学的传统工具。琉善却以对话为"硬件"，以修辞学为"软件"，将糅合了二者特点的讽刺对话，应用于对社会病态现象的批评。他不同于同时

---

[1] Barry Baldwin, *Studies in Lucian*, Toronto: A. M. Hakkert Ltd., 1973, p. 9; Jones, C. P., *Culture and Society in Lucian*, Cambridge: Harvard University Press, 1986, p. 14.

四、罗马与东汉宗教批判思想之比较

代的其他文人。[1]其作品个性鲜明,虽模仿古典著作,但却是旧瓶新酒,承载了作者的原创思想。

王充和琉善,一个成长在东方的古代中国的东汉王朝;一个生活在西方的古罗马帝国安敦尼王朝。文化背景的巨大差异不言而喻。二者在关注重点、写作风格和论证方法等方面也各有特点。但二者的宗教批判思想,根据其作品内容却都可以分为批评祭祀、否定巫祝、批判传说三个方面。其中,祭祀分为向神献祭和向人献祭两类;巫祝则包含了求取预言和破解神力两类;传言涉及世俗民众和知识分子两个群体。由此可见,这两位表面上截然不同的学者,竟具有极为相似的宗教批判思想。

---

[1] Alfred Croiset, Maurice Croiset, *An Abridged History of Greek Literature*, translated by George F. Heffelbower, A. M., London: Macmillan Company, 1904, p. 542. 克鲁瓦塞认为:琉善是希腊天才几乎不再具有创新性的时期出现的唯一具有独创思想的思想家。(Alfred Croiset, Maurice Croiset, *An Abridged History of Greek Literature*, p. 542.) "这一时期我们能够遇到的唯一伟大的名字就是琉善。"(Alfred Croiset, Maurice Croiset, *An Abridged History of Greek Literature*, p. 519.) 科瓦略夫在其著作《古代罗马史》中将琉善和普鲁塔克并称为当时"两位具有世界声名的作家",并称赞他终于能够克服"'诡辩术'并成为古典时期的最后一位伟大的讽刺作家。"([俄]科瓦略夫:《古代罗马史》,王以铸译,上海:上海书店出版社,2007,第736页,第737页)

以主张预言无益为例。人生活于世上,与外在的人类社会和自然界总不可避免地发生接触和碰撞。在这个过程中有众多因素人力无法掌控,诸多结果让人不愿接纳。英国社会人类学家马林诺夫斯基(B. Malinowski)指出,针对无能为力的事情,人们会诉诸于巫术。"他们的经验及理智告诉他们劳力和理智有限的程度,而另一方面他们相信巫术可以帮助他们。"[1] 因此无论是古代东方还是西方,人们都试图依靠预言知晓未来,或用魔法破除祸患,来达到趋利避害的目的。这些行为是古代宗教的重要组成部分,同样也是琉善和王充批判的重点之一。

在《被盘问的宙斯》中,琉善笔下的昔尼斯科斯说:"既然人们完全无力做出改变,那么提前预知未来没有什么好处。难道你认为一个人提前知道自己将死在铁矛头之下,就能够靠把自己关起来逃过一劫?这是不可能的,因为命运女神会引他出去打猎,将他带到矛尖前。"[2] 琉善在《泽莫纳克斯》中,也表达

---

[1] 〔英〕马林诺夫斯基:《文化论》,费孝通等译,北京:中国民间文艺出版社,1987,第55—56页。

[2] Lucian, *Zeus Catechized*, 12.

了类似的意思。琉善在转述他所欣赏的泽莫纳克斯（Demonax）的事迹时，曾写过这样一段话："泽莫纳克斯看到一个预言家公开进行预测以赚取钱财，他说：'我看不出你收取这些费用的理由是什么——如果你认为你有能力改变命运，那你收的钱就太少了；如果一切都是上天注定的，无法改变，那你的预言又有什么用呢？'"[1] 再者，预言不仅无法为人解忧，还会给人带来更多的困惑。在《演悲剧的宙斯》中，当宙斯命阿波罗预言人间两个辩论的哲学家谁会赢时，阿波罗的神谕是：

"请听预言者阿波罗的宣示吧，
关于一场令人胆寒的争吵，
絮叨言辞当武器，忽低忽高，
激烈战斗不间断，狂呼尖叫，
这边那边，震动尖尖的耕犁柄。
当弯爪的秃鹫捕捉飞蝗的时候，
唤雨的乌鸦发出最后一声嘎嘎。

---

[1] Lucian, *Demonax*, 37.

保守抑或包容

驴子踢了它的巧女儿,胜利属于骡子。"[1]

这条神谕始终在东拉西扯,完全没给出任何有效信息。因此,琉善在文中的代言人摩摩斯(Momus)说:"宙斯啊,听到这么清楚明了的预言,我怎能不笑呢?"[2]而他所谓的"明了"指的是:"……这个神示清楚地告诉我们,这个家伙是个骗子,而你们这些相信他的人则愚蠢而顽固,笨得连蚱蜢都不如。"[3]在此文中另一处,琉善谈到了克洛索斯(Croesus)的悲剧[4],借伊壁鸠鲁派哲学家达弥斯(Damis)之口讥讽德尔菲神庙的神谕,批评阿波罗的神示如同赫尔墨斯的脸一样,从哪个角度看都可以。[5]另外,在《诸神对话》中,赫拉与勒托(Leto)对话时说:"阿波罗装作无所

---

[1] 〔古罗马〕琉善:《琉善哲学文选》,罗念生、陈洪文、王焕生等译,北京:商务印书馆,1980,第182页。

[2] Lucian, *Zeus Rants*, 31.

[3] Lucian, *Zeus Rants*, 31.

[4] 克洛索斯欲与波斯开战,战前得到德尔菲神谕为:如果克洛索斯进攻波斯人,便可以灭掉一个大国。克洛索斯以为神谕所指的大国为波斯,没想到是自己国破人亡。参见《琉善哲学文选》,第176页,注释2。

[5] Lucian, *Zeus Rants*, 43.

不通，不论是箭术、竖琴，还是医药、预言。他在德尔菲、克拉洛斯（Claros）、克罗丰（Colophon）和狄狄玛（Didyma）设置神示所，用虚假的答复和模棱两可的回答欺骗他的主顾，以规避犯错的风险。他由此聚敛了很多钱财，因为有大批蠢人甘愿来被他骗。然而，有智慧的人看穿了他的故弄玄虚。这个预言家，他不知道自己会用那个铁环打死自己的爱人，也没能预见到以他的美貌和长发，达芙妮（Daphne）居然会逃开他。"[1] 琉善通过上述内容批评了神谕的模糊性和欺骗性，讽刺了太阳神阿波罗终日为他人发布预言，却对自己未来的命运一无所知。

在预言方面，琉善批判的另一个重要对象是假预言者亚历山大。琉善在《亚历山大——假预言者》中详述了骗子亚历山大的斑斑劣迹，戳穿了他制造的种种骗局，用很多事例证明所谓"神谕"之可笑。例如，儒提里阿努斯（Rutilianus）询问自己继承了谁的灵魂时，得到的答案是："最初你为珀琉斯之子；其后是米南德，现在是你当下模样，此后你会化作一道阳

---

[1] Lucian, *Dialogues of the Gods*, 244.

光。你一百岁之后还能有八十年的寿龄。"[1]然而,此人七十岁的时候就去世了。又如,一个人问亚历山大自己应该给正青春年少的儿子请一个什么样的老师。亚历山大给出的神示说:"成为毕达哥拉斯;啊,还有那位优秀的诗人[2],写作战争者。"[3]谁知几天后这孩子就死了。于是,神示的谎言被事实揭穿。琉善的作品让人们看到,这个当时受到广泛推崇的预言家,其真实面目竟是这般模样:"信口雌黄、诡计多端、背信弃义、心肠歹毒;华而不实、厚颜无耻、胆大妄为、无恶不作、口蜜腹剑、花言巧语、虚情假意、矫饰伪行。"[4]琉善对亚历山大的攻击和讽刺毫不留情。他说要讲述亚历山大的各种诡计和骗局,比清理奥吉厄斯的牛舍(Augean Stables)还困难。在他眼中,亚历山大比强盗还野蛮,就连讲述他的故事都令人感到羞愧。[5]

琉善还在文中指出,"神示"造成的恶果不仅令

---

[1] Lucian, *Alexander the False Prophet*, 34.
[2] "诗人"指荷马。参见《琉善哲学文选》,第235页,注释1。
[3] Lucian, *Alexander the False Prophet*, 33.
[4] Lucian, *Alexander the False Prophet*, 4.
[5] Lucian, *Alexander the False Prophet*, 1–2.

四、罗马与东汉宗教批判思想之比较

人损失钱财,甚至可能会伤人性命,危及国运。亚历山大曾怂恿塞威里阿努斯(Severianus)进攻亚美尼亚(Armenia),结果导致塞威里阿努斯及其军队全部被消灭。[1] 在日耳曼战争期间,当元首奥理略准备与马克曼尼人和夸德人作战时,亚历山大发出神示:

"我命令你们把库柏勒女神的两个侍者——
山上养大的走兽[2] 和印度气候培育的
各种香花香草扔到天上降下的
雨水形成的河流伊斯特洛斯的漩涡里,
那就会获得胜利、荣誉和可爱的和平。"[3]

然而,当罗马人根据这条神谕的指使将狮子和香草扔入伊斯特洛斯河,狮子却游到了对岸敌人那里,

---

[1] Lucian, *Alexander the False Prophet*, 27. 帕提亚人对亚美尼亚的王位继承问题进行干涉。小亚细亚东部卡帕多细亚省的罗马总督塞威里阿努斯,于161年带一小股军队进入亚美尼亚,结果惨败。(Lucian, *Lucian*, Vol. Ⅳ, Loeb Classical Library, Cambridge, Massachusetts: Harvard University Press, 1925, p.213, note 2.)

[2] 即狮子。

[3] 〔古罗马〕琉善:《琉善哲学文选》,第241页。

被蛮族人当作奇怪的狗或者狼打死了,而罗马军队大败,损失惨重。

面对预言失败,亚历山大极力粉饰自己的错误,厚颜无耻地拿克洛索斯的故事为自己开脱,妄言神示只是说会有胜利与和平出现,但并未讲明谁是胜利者。这两次荒唐的预言给罗马帝国造成了巨大的损失。除了上述直接影响外,琉善的作品还将迷信活动对政治生活产生的隐性影响揭露了出来。例如,琉善在《亚历山大——假预言者》中说:"如果在拆开和阅读那些呈上来的卷轴[1]时,他看到一些危险或大胆的问题,便会将它们扣下不送回去,让提问者受制于他,因恐惧而成为他的奴隶,因为他们知道自己都问了些什么。你也知道特别富有和有权势的人爱问什么问题。"[2]由此可见,作为神的代言人,迷信活动的组织者往往可以掌握统治阶层内部不为人知的秘密。对秘密的掌控,就等于对人的掌控。这说明宗教迷信是一只隐形的手,在幕后悄然影响着国家的命运。这一隐患在琉善的作品中被揭示了出来。

---

[1] 卷轴内写的是问卜者向神灵提的问题。
[2] Lucian, *Alexander the False Prophet*, 32.

四、罗马与东汉宗教批判思想之比较

《说文解字》卜部:"占,视兆也,从卜口。"[1]可见占卜,本质上是要获知预兆的行为。如伏尔泰言:"占卜吉凶,预言未来,也属于神谕一类,而且我认为年代更为古老。"[2]中国汉代就流行卜筮这种古老的占卜活动。跟琉善一样,王充也认为占卜该受到批判。他在《卜筮》中批判了关于占卜算卦的迷信活动。王充所探讨的卜筮与古罗马人向神灵求取预言相似,是中国古人向他们的神——"天""地"提问。"卜"是占卜者向天提问;"筮"是占卜者向地提问。蓍草和龟甲是卜筮常用的工具,人们认为天、地用龟兆和蓍数来回答占卜者的问题。王充指出:"如实论之,卜筮不问天地,蓍龟未必神灵。"[3](《论衡·卜筮》)也就是说,蓍草和龟甲也不一定灵通,卜筮不能达到问天地的目的。

首先,王充根据孔子与子路的对话,提出蓍草和龟甲并无实际效应,只因"蓍"字意为生存时间长,

---

[1] 许慎:《说文解字》,北京:中华书局,1963,第70页。
[2] 〔法〕伏尔泰:《风俗论》(上),梁守锵译,北京:商务印书馆,1994,第129页。
[3] 黄晖:《论衡校释》(三),北京:中华书局,1990,第998页。

"龟"字意为年代久,"明狐疑之事,当问耆旧也"[1]。(《论衡·卜筮》)表示有疑问应请教年长者。可见蓍草和龟甲没有什么神通,因而也就不能用来向天地提问了。另外,王充指出天地有形体所以能运动。能运动的,就是有生命。按照人类活动的道理来看,对活人有问题就必须问活人。现在天地有生命,但蓍草、龟甲是死的。对有生命的天、地有疑问,却通过死的蓍草、龟甲提问,如何能得到答复呢?再者,如果卜筮真的是一种向天地提问的方式,而兆数也真的是天地的回答的话,那么现实中就不应该如此:"人道,相问则对,不问不应。无求,空扣人之门;无问,虚辨人之前,则主人笑而不应,或怒而不对。试使卜筮之人,空钻龟而卜,虚揲蓍而筮,戏弄天地,亦得兆数,天地妄应乎?又试使人骂天而卜,欧地而筮,无道至甚,亦得兆数。苟谓兆数天地之神,何不灭其火,灼其手,振其指而乱其数,使之身体疾痛,血气凑硔?而犹为之见兆出数,何天地之不惮劳,用心不恶也?"[2](《论衡·卜筮》)也就是说,不管是让卜筮者毫无目的地占

---

[1] 黄晖:《论衡校释》(三),第999页。
[2] 黄晖:《论衡校释》(三),第1001页。

四、罗马与东汉宗教批判思想之比较

卜,或者占卜的时候辱骂天地,都一样会得到兆数,既没出现不得结果的情况,也不存在占卜者受惩罚的现象。

其次,王充又论证了问卜是行不通的。他提出,如果对天有疑问,那就要向天提问。可是天有形体、耳朵吗?如果有,天那么高,耳朵那么远,怎么能够听到人的提问?如果没有形体,那么也就没有耳、口,无法告诉人答案。况且天道自然,不可能有意识地回答人的提问。同时,正如王充在其他地方经常做的那个比喻,人之于天,就像虮虱之于人。人那么渺小,天地那么遥远、巨大,人的提问是无法传到天地的耳朵的。至于有人提出的"人怀天地之气。天地之气,在形体之中,神明是矣。人将卜筮,告令蓍龟,则神以耳闻口言。若己思念,神明从胸腹之中闻知其旨,故钻龟揲蓍,兆见数著"[1]。(《论衡·卜筮》)意思是人都怀有天地之气,神明就是这气了,可以借助人的口、耳,通过人的胸腹了解人的疑问,然后钻龟揲蓍,显现兆数。王充反驳道:如果按照这个逻辑,就

---

[1] 黄晖:《论衡校释》(三),第1000页。

不应该出现占卜之时，人心中有一个预想，但占卜的结果与其预想相反的情况了。因为"夫思虑者，己之神也；为兆数者，亦己之神。一身之神，在胸中为思虑，在胸外为兆数，犹人入户而坐，出门而行也。行坐不异意，出入不易情"[1]。(《论衡·卜筮》)意思是说，思想应当与行动保持一致，如果心中所思是神灵所想，而兆数又是神灵想法的具体体现，那么兆数就应该与人的预想相一致。

在古罗马，预言会对国家大事产生影响，在古代中国也是如此。其中最典型的就是王充所批判的谶纬之学。纬，是对儒家经典的解读；谶，是神的预言。《四库全书总目提要》中说："案儒者多称'谶纬'，其实谶自谶，纬自纬，非一类也。谶者，诡为隐语，预决吉凶；《史记·秦本纪》，称卢生奏録图书之语，是其始也。纬者，经之支流，衍及旁义。"[2] "严格地说，谶与纬并非一类。但是，纬书必须编造谶文预言才能显得更神圣，谶语必须依傍儒家经义才能更令人信服。于是二

---

[1] 黄晖：《论衡校释》(三)，第1000页。
[2] 永瑢等：《四库全书总目提要》(二)，北京：商务印书馆，1933，第62页。

四、罗马与东汉宗教批判思想之比较

者逐渐合流,很难严格区分。"[1]谶纬之学在汉代广泛流行,上至皇帝、百官,下至黎民百姓,都信奉谶纬之说。"谶纬的核心内容是政治思想,主要讨论'受命之符'、'皇道帝德'等天下治乱、国家兴衰、政教得失、君臣离合等。纬书、谶文大多涉及最为敏感的政治权力合法性问题,因而受到朝野上下的广泛关注。"[2]例如,传说孔子死前预言:"不知何一男子,自谓秦始皇,上我之堂,踞我之床,颠倒我的衣裳,至沙丘而亡"[3];(《论衡·实知》)再如,有种预言说:"亡秦者,胡也。"[4](《论衡·实知》)都是典型的谶语。第一条谶语预言秦始皇的出现和死亡;第二条预言秦二世胡亥亡国。针对这些谶语的内容,王充都进行了详细的批判。[5]他在《实知》中说:"谶书秘文,远见未然,空虚暗昧,豫睹未有,达闻暂见,卓谲怪神,若非庸口所能言。"[6](《论衡·实知》)意思是,谶纬图书,言辞含

---

[1] 张鸿、张分田:《王充》,昆明:云南教育出版社,2009,第94页。
[2] 张鸿、张分田:《王充》,第94页。
[3] 黄晖:《论衡校释》(四),第1069页。
[4] 黄晖:《论衡校释》(四),第1070页。
[5] 王充在《论衡·实知》中对谶语进行了批判。
[6] 黄晖:《论衡校释》(四),第1072页。

糊晦涩，宣称能够预见未来，让人乍一听感觉神秘古怪，好像不是寻常人能说出来的话。王充表示，事实上谶纬之说多是凭空编造，或故意扭曲前人的言论，绝对不可信。[1]

王充跟琅善一样，也将讨论的焦点转向了占卜预言者本人。他说："世人言卜筮者多，得实诚者寡。"[2]（《论衡·卜筮》）即世上谈占卜的人很多，但真正会解读兆数的人很少。用龟甲和蓍草进行占卜，兆数就会出现。但由于占卜者并不懂如何解释，所以占卜结果吉凶难辨。王充以武王伐纣和鲁将伐越时进行的两次占卜为例，论证了"周多子贡直占之知，寡若孔子诡论之材，故睹非常之兆，不能审也"[3]。（《论衡·卜筮》）意为：周代人多像子贡那样只知僵化地解释兆数，很少有孔子那样出众的论证能力。[4] 既然占卜者都不能对卜筮结果作出准确的解释，那让人们如何相信卜筮

---

[1] 张鸿、张分田：《王充》，第97页。

[2] 黄晖：《论衡校释》（三），第1003页。

[3] 黄晖：《论衡校释》（三），第1005页。

[4] 事实上，王充此时从自然命定论出发，认为占卜结果的吉凶会和人命的善恶相逢遇，又在一定程度上肯定了卜筮结果的准确性。这是其疾虚妄不够彻底的表现，此处暂不作细致论述。

能够给予他们正确的答案呢？

最后，如琉善所说的，若人类的命运无法改变，那么占卜预言又有什么意义呢？王充始终秉持自然命定论，主张人因天地之气而诞生，自出生之时便因承受的气厚薄不同，而形成各自不同的"命"。人的一切富贵贫贱，适逢遭遇皆由"命"决定，"人必须服从或不得不服从"[1]。就像《命禄》中所说的："凡人遇偶及遭累害，皆由命也。有死生寿夭之命，亦有贵贱贫富之命。自王公逮庶人，圣贤及下愚，凡有首目之类，含血之属，莫不有命。"[2]（《论衡·命禄》）既然一切都已命中注定，通过卜筮去向天地请教还有什么用处呢？即便知道问题的答案，人们又能做什么呢？"命则不可勉，时则不可力，知者归之于天，故坦荡恬忽。"[3]（《论衡·命禄》）命运是不能勉强改变的，时运也不是努力就能得到的。因此，去预测或试图采取行动都是徒劳，倒不如学聪明人，接受现实，求得一份恬淡释然的心境。

---

[1] 邓红：《王充新八论》，北京：中国社会科学出版社，2003，第64页。
[2] 黄晖：《论衡校释》（一），第20页。
[3] 黄晖：《论衡校释》（一），第20页。

通过对比我们可以看到,琉善与王充都认为预言无益,在论证过程中二者都指出预言的言辞含糊晦涩,预言者也并不可信,对于影响国家政事的预言都提出了批评,也均论证了既然命运无法改变,那么占卜、预言都是没有意义的。除此之外,以同样的方式还可以证明,琉善和王充在主张向神祭祀无补,人死即无知觉,巫祝无力扭转乾坤,迷信传言荒诞愚人等方面,也存在着诸多相似之处。这些都反映出两位学者都具有强烈的理性精神和明确的宗教批判态度。

(三)弃用不等于迫害

琉善和王充的宗教批判思想都不是凭空生成,均有其深刻的社会和文化根源。他们二人都生活在古代世界,那是一个信仰与政治深刻交融的时代。

"琉善恰好出生在一个迷信盛行、神迹风靡的时代,……这个时代的领袖都十分虔诚。元首马尔库斯·奥勒留认为没有神,生命就没有意义;元首妻子福斯蒂娜生病的时候,弗隆托终日为其祈祷,望她早日康复;小普林尼修建了两座神庙;狄奥·克里索斯托姆（Dion Chrysostom）、普鲁塔克和爱比克泰德（Epictetus）都是有神论者。他们都坚信神灵干预人类事务。"[1] 如 F. G. 埃利森所言："在安敦尼王朝这一伟大的时代，迷信（不论是本土还是东方的），都在罗马帝国和煦的阳光下，伴随着由元首身体力行所推广的高尚的哲学蓬勃发展。"[2] 2 世纪罗马帝国对传统宗教十分重视。罗马政府与罗马宗教是联合在一起的。[3] 神灵的任务是保护国家和使国家强大；而祭司则是组织祭祀神灵的公共官员。[4] 正如吉本所说，"他们（罗马统治者）了解并重视宗教的价值，因为它与公民政府紧密相连。他们鼓励公共节日，这种节日可以教化民众的行为。他们将占卜技艺当作推行政策的便利工具"[5]。

[1] W. L. Hime, *Lucian the Syrian Satirist*, London, New York and Bombay：Longmans, Green, and Co., 1900, pp. 27–28.

[2] F.G. Allinson, *Lucian*, *Satirist and Artist*, Boston：Marshall Jones Company, 1926, p. 89.

[3] Edited by Sarah Iles Johnston, *Ancient Religions*, Cambridge：The Belknap Press of Harvard University Press, 2007, p. 228.

[4] Don S. Armentrout, "Book Reviews：*The State*, *Law*, *and Religion*：*Pagan Rome*, by Alan Watson", *Church History*, Vol. 63, No. 2, p. 250.

[5] Edward Gibbon, *History of the Decline and Fall of the Roman Empire*, Penguin Classics, Middlesex：Viking Penguin Inc., 1981, p. 54.

因此宗教信仰是当时罗马统治阶层关注的核心问题，甚至是其矛盾的主要焦点。[1] 而琉善却对古希腊罗马传统宗教展开了毫不留情的批判。从内容上看，他抨击祭祀，批评预言，讽刺神灵；从方法上看，他采用了嘲笑讥讽的手法；从工具上看，他以各种哲学理念为武器。在琉善犀利的笔锋下，一切玄幻的事物都无所遁逃。然而，对施政工具的攻击，并没有让琉善遭到政府的迫害。他四处游历、演说，与罗马上层交好，甚至晚年还在埃及担任官职，负责的工作是："做诉讼案件的开庭和准备工作；记录所有语言和行为；在辩护人讲话时给予其引导；如实记录长官的决意，确保其准确、清晰，并将之放入公务档案中永久保存。"[2] 他在从事这些工作的时候得到的薪金也很高，并对于自己的工作倍感荣耀，而且表示对未来的发展充满期望。

琉善所生活的时代被 J. B. 伯里（J. B. Bury）称为

---

[1] James B. Rives, "Graeco-Roman Religion in the Roman Empire: Old Assumptions and New Approaches", *Currents in Biblical Research*, Vol. 8, No. 2(2010), p.249.

[2] Lucian, *Apology for the "Salaried Posts in Great Houses"*, 12.

四、罗马与东汉宗教批判思想之比较

"理性自由时代"。"罗马的政策一般来说是对整个罗马境内的各种宗教和各种言论都采取宽容的态度。渎神并没有受到惩罚。在提比略皇帝（元首）的箴言中表达了这个原则：'要是诸神受到侮辱，让他们自己去处理吧。'"[1] 当时的罗马帝国对于言论没有过多限制。事实上，琉善对传统宗教的批判，也并不是出现在罗马帝国的一个新现象，而是可以追溯到前苏格拉底哲学家。[2] 从前苏格拉底哲学家到亚里士多德，哲学与传统宗教似乎一直以来都是不相容的。对传统宗教的批判，源自哲学的思想属于在古希腊的一直并行的两大精神分类中的一类——"事实上，在希腊有着两种倾向，一种是热情的、宗教的、神秘的、出世的，另一种是欢愉的、经验的、理性的，并且是对获得多种多样事实的知识感到兴趣的。希罗多德就代表后一种倾向；最早的伊奥尼亚哲学家们也是如此；亚里

---

[1] 〔英〕J. B. 伯里：《思想自由史》，第22页。

[2] Pieter de Villiers, "Interpreting the New Testament in the Light of Pagan Criticisms of Oracles and Prophecies in Greco-Roman Times", *Neotestamentica*, Vol. 33, No. 1 (1999), p. 48.

士多德在一定限度内也是如此"[1]。因此,古代的哲学家,都不是传统宗教的忠实信徒。例如,在前苏格拉底哲学家当中,普罗泰戈拉就在《神论》中明确对神的存在表示质疑:"至于神,我没有把握说他们存在或者他们不存在,也不敢说他们是什么样子;因为有许多妨碍了我们确切的知识,例如问题的晦涩与人生的短促。"[2] 至古典时期,亚里士多德的"神"与希腊罗马传统宗教的神灵也截然不同,"他认为,神是超时间的存在,是完美的,是纯粹思想、幸福和完全的自我实现。……神是只有形式没有质料[3]的"[4];"神就是纯粹的思想,就是完美"[5];"有一种既永恒又不动而且独立于可感觉的事物之外的实质。也已经证明了这种实

---

[1] 〔英〕罗素:《西方哲学史》(上),何兆武、李约瑟译,北京:商务印书馆,1982,第46页。

[2] 〔英〕罗素:《西方哲学史》(上),何兆武、李约瑟译,第111页。

[3] 〔英〕罗素:《西方哲学史》(上),何兆武、李约瑟译,第215页:"用亚里士多德的例子,如果一个人制造了一个铜球,那末铜便是质料,球便是形式;以平静的海为例,水便是质料,平静便是形式。"

[4] 〔英〕罗素:《西方哲学史》,张作成译,北京:北京出版社,2007,第42页。

[5] 〔英〕罗素:《西方哲学史》,张作成译,北京:北京出版社,2007,第42页。

四、罗马与东汉宗教批判思想之比较

质不能有任何大小,而是既不包含许多部分,又是不可分割的……并且也已经证明了它是无感觉的、不可移动的"。[1] 而伊壁鸠鲁虽然相信神是存在的,但主张神不干涉人类事务,[2] 反对世人对巫术、占卜的痴迷。[3] 到了罗马帝国时期,对传统宗教,特别是占卜的批判,也并非只琉善一人为之。西塞罗在他的《论占卜》(*De Divinatione*)中也反对占卜,理由是占卜终难摆脱虚假和诡计。[4] 而且他还观察到德尔菲神谕已不再发挥作用,并以此作为反驳神谕的论据。[5]

因此,我们可以看到,知识分子对传统宗教的不推崇,并非始于琉善。这一传统在西方自古便如此。大多数哲学家都是一边拒绝着传统信仰,一边参与着

---

[1] 〔英〕罗素:《西方哲学史》(上),何兆武、李约瑟译,第219页。

[2] 〔英〕罗素:《西方哲学史》(上),何兆武、李约瑟译,第313页。

[3] 〔英〕罗素:《西方哲学史》(上),何兆武、李约瑟译,第314页:"由于他们抗议晚期异教徒对巫术、占星与通神的日益增长的信奉,他们也算做了有用的事"。

[4] Pieter de Villiers, "Interpreting the New Testament in the Light of Pagan Criticisms of Oracles and Prophecies in Greco-Roman Times", p. 42.

[5] Pieter de Villiers, "Interpreting the New Testament in the Light of Pagan Criticisms of Oracles and Prophecies in Greco-Roman Times", p. 44.

传统祭祀活动。[1]但信仰的不虔诚,并没有给哲学家们带来严重的迫害。另外,琉善所在罗马的元首马尔库斯·奥勒留(公元121年—180年),是当时斯多葛派哲学的代表人物。换句话说,琉善生在了哲学家担任元首的时代。马尔库斯·奥勒留本人作为哲学家,知道思想与行动的差别,[2]理解哲学信仰与参与日常宗教活动是可以兼得的。在这样的文化氛围下,知识分子可以享有较宽松的思想自由空间,存在琉善这样的学者不足为怪。

通过比较我们看到,王充与琉善有着同样理性的批判精神,他们都反对祭神、祀鬼,批评占卜、解除,反驳流言、禁忌。胡适先生说,中国古代宗教,约有三个要点:"(一)是一个有意志知觉,能赏善罚恶的

---

[1] 因为传统宗教渗透在世俗生活的方方面面,无可回避。具体论述,参见拙作《审视与反思:琉善眼中的神灵》,载《北京师范大学学报(社会科学版)》,2015,第2期,第89页。

[2] 〔英〕罗素:《西方哲学史》(上),何兆武、李约瑟译,第330—331页:"他(马尔库斯·奥勒留)的《沉思集》一书是为他自己而写的,显然是并不准备发表;这部书表明了他感到自己的公共职责的负担沉重,并且还为一种极大的厌倦所苦恼着。……在一系列必须加以抗拒的各种世俗的欲望里,他感到其中最具有吸引力的一种就是想要隐退去过一个宁静的乡村生活的那种愿望。"可见马尔库斯·奥勒留本人就经历着精神世界与现实世界之间的冲突。

四、罗马与东汉宗教批判思想之比较

天帝;(二)是崇拜自然界种种质力迷信,如祭天地日月山川之类;(三)是鬼神的迷信,以为人死有知,能作祸福,故必须祭礼供养他们。这几种迷信,可算得是古中国的国教。这个国教的教主即是'天子'。"[3] 而王充却针对"天有知觉,能赏罚"的观点,展开了全面而持续的批判。事实上,王充并非此举的开创者,类似的反思在中国古代哲学史上有着久远的传统。早在春秋时期,老子就针对旧有的天道观念,即把天看作一个有意识、知喜怒的万物主宰,进行批判,提出"天道不仁"[4]。至荀子之时,对"无意志的天"的论证已达到很高的水平。他不仅能用老子的"天道不仁"来修

---

[3] 胡适:《中国哲学史大纲》,北京:商务印书馆,2011,第319页。

[4] 胡适:《中国哲学史大纲》,第42页:"这仁字有两种说法:第一,仁是慈爱的意思。这是最明白的解说。王弼说'地不为兽生刍而兽食刍,不为人生狗而人食狗。无为于万物,而万物各适其所用。'这是把不仁作无有恩意解。第二,仁即是'人'的意思。《中庸》说:'仁者,人也';《孟子》说:'仁也者,人也';刘熙《释名》说:'人,仁也;仁,生物也';不仁便是说不是人,不和人同类。古代把天看作有意志、有知识、能喜怒的主宰,是把天看作人同类,这叫做天人同类说(Anthropomorphism)。老子的'天地不仁'说,似乎也含有天地不与人同性的意思。人性之中,以慈爱为最普通,故说天地不与人同类,即是说天地无有恩意。老子这一观念,打破古典天人同类的谬说,立下后来自然哲学的基础。"

正儒家的"赏善罚恶"的有意志的天,还能"免去老子、庄子天道观念的安命守旧的种种恶果"。[1]荀子将天道放在一边,注重人治,鼓励人们"征服天行以为人用"[2]。

自汉至晋的哲学家的思想,都以古代诸子哲学为起点。[3]王充思想的产生自是受到前人成果的影响,故而会有天人无感的主张。但一个人思想的形成,还与其所处时代有很大关系。正如老子反对旧天道说,是因为他"生在那种纷争大乱的时代,眼见杀人、破家、灭国等等惨祸,以为若有一个有意志知觉的天帝,绝不致有这种惨祸"。[4]而王充反对儒家的天人感应论,是因为其所在的东汉王朝豪门士族阶层迅速膨胀,"垄断特权,兼并土地,不仅与广大农民矛盾尖锐,而且也引起了庶族地主的强烈不满,酝酿着新的社会危机"。[5]在这种情况下,东汉统治者试图宣扬"天人感应"的理论以达到强化统治的目的。在该理论的指

---

[1] 胡适:《中国哲学史大纲》,第250页。
[2] 胡适:《中国哲学史大纲》,第250页。
[3] 胡适:《中国哲学史大纲》,导言第5页。
[4] 胡适:《中国哲学史大纲》,第41页。
[5] 王充撰,陈蒲清点校:《论衡》,前言第1页。

四、罗马与东汉宗教批判思想之比较

导下,宗教迷信、谶纬之学广泛流行,民众受到愚惑。王充对此深感担忧,认为应该秉承"事实疾妄"[1]的精神对上述现象加以批判。

"天人感应"是东汉大一统王朝巩固统治的哲学基础,是掌控民众、统一思想的重要工具。朝廷对于种种占卜、祭祀等活动也大力支持。人君的统治理念与奉天为人格神的迷信思想,紧密地交织在一起。"如果说包括全部习俗和见解主张在内的社会结构是与宗教信仰密切联系在一起,并被认为是受到神的庇护的,那么对社会秩序的批评就意味着不虔诚,而对宗教信仰的批评则是对超自然力量的天罚神谴的直接挑战了。"[2]反过来,对天罚神谴的挑战,也就是对统治理念的批判。而王充的作品就是对天罚神谴的直接挑战。那么,伴随着他的挑战,受到质疑的必然是东汉王朝的统治理念。

世人多认为,古代中国自汉代起便"罢黜百家,独尊儒术",推行文化专制政策。在这种政策下,知

---

[1] 黄晖:《论衡校释》(四),第1185页。
[2] 〔英〕J. B. 伯里:《思想自由史》,周颖如译,第2页。

识分子遭到严重的迫害。[1] 人们常用的例子，就是尹敏和桓谭等人的故事。然而，这些事件应当从政治的角度，而非从思想的角度，去考虑。《后汉书·儒林列传》载："帝以敏博通经记，令校图谶，使蠲去崔发所为王莽着录次比。敏对曰：'谶书非圣人所作，其中多近鄙别字，颇类世俗之辞，恐疑误后生。'帝不纳。敏因其阙文增之曰：'君无口，为汉辅。'帝见而怪之，召敏问其故。敏对曰：'臣见前人增损图书，敢不自量，窃幸万一。'帝深非之，虽竟不罪，而亦以此沉滞。"[2] 尹敏曾在皇帝面前明确表达自己反对谶纬的思想，但并未因对谶书有异议或者篡改谶书而获罪，只因他与中央态度不符而未继续得到重用而已。他后来被关押免官是因为受到了周虑的牵连："永平五年，诏书捕男子周虑。虑素有名称，而善于敏，敏坐系免官。"[3] 可见，对于东汉统治者而言，政治问题远比思想重要。

至于桓谭因主张反对谶纬而险遭处斩，也并非因

---

[1] "由于涉及皇权尊严，谁公开反对谶纬、符瑞之说，谁就有罢官杀头、株连九族的危险。"（张鸿、张分田：《王充》，第92页。）

[2] 范晔撰，李贤等注：《后汉书》（第九册），北京：中华书局，1965，第2558页。

[3] 范晔撰，李贤等注：《后汉书》（第九册），第2559页。

四、罗马与东汉宗教批判思想之比较

其秉承异类的思想、对谶纬之说不够笃信，而是因他公然反对朝廷的文化方针，即对权力和政策的直接挑战。东汉初，光武帝刘秀就很重视使用谶纬来稳定自己的统治，《后汉书·张衡列传》中说他"善谶"[1]。桓谭与刘秀之间的矛盾，是政治理念上的冲突。这种不协调早在刘秀即位之初就已经显现出来了："世祖即位，征待诏，上书言事失旨，不用。"[2] 可见桓谭刚刚上任之时上疏提出的政见就不合皇帝心意。后来他又两次上疏直谏，尖锐地指出皇帝不应信赖谶语，以及用兵赏赐不够的问题，更加引起皇帝的不满。而此后在讨论灵台位置时，皇帝问桓谭关于用谶语来决定位置的意见，则更像是有意为之。刘秀明知桓谭对谶语的看法，还依然引他阐述谶书并非经典的道理，后又以"桓谭非圣无法"为由而要将其处斩。这样的冲突，显然并不是皇帝要在思想上限制知识分子，而是政治家与士人治国理念矛盾尖锐化的结果，并不能用来证明汉代对文人的思想控制，或说明朝廷对知识分子予以极少的思想自由空间。

---

[1] 范晔撰，李贤等注:《后汉书》(第七册)，第1911页。
[2] 范晔撰，李贤等注:《后汉书》(第四册)，第956页。

保守抑或包容

与此同时，回顾王充的生平和思想，他并没有因其理性的精神和战斗的文字而遭遇不幸。虽然仕途并不坦荡，但毕竟也曾涉足宦海，四度入仕。这就表示他并没有为统治阶层所抛弃，更没有受到严重迫害。不仅如此，他还讲课办学，将自己的思想传播出去。在第一次退隐后，王充便"归乡里，屏居教授"[1]。"教学生，王充同样贯彻自己'实事疾妄'的精神，努力给他们传授真实有用的东西，对世俗流行的许多'虚妄之语'加以澄清。"[2] 更值得注意的是，王充在晚年，《论衡》已然著成，开始流传时，居然还收到了汉章帝下发的"特诏公车征"，而且此次等待他的官职较此前四次出任的职位还要更高，可以在天子左右为官。当然，王充得以善终或许也与其写作的《齐世》《宣汉》等篇有关，不过这也进一步反映了对汉代统治者而言，政治立场重于思想统一。若先秦诸子百家争鸣，没有受到迫害是因为尚无一个大一统的中央集权，那么在东汉强化中央统治，以及罢黜百家、独尊儒术的政策

---

[1] 范晔撰，李贤等注：《后汉书》（第六册），第1629页。
[2] 徐斌：《论衡之人——王充传》，杭州：浙江人民出版社，2005，第116—117页。

下，王充依然可以全身而退，则更是说明了当时的政权没有对知识分子实施严酷的打压。

同样是批判为统治阶层所重视的传统宗教，攻击官方政策赖以执行的工具，琉善和王充都没有受到来自政府的直接打击，也都在各自思想已然形成并传播出去之后，在晚年还能获得官职。王充在东汉时期的生存环境，竟与琉善在"理性自由时代"的罗马所得到的相似。这些都表明，东汉王朝的文化政策，给了文人思想以相对自由的空间，而并未像以往学者所提出的那样，用腥风血雨来压制文人的行为，禁锢他们的思维。

参考资料

[1] 吴虞:《儒家主张阶级制度之害》，载《新青年》，1917，第3卷第4号。

[2] 陈独秀:《宪法与孔教》，载《新青年》，1916，第2卷第3号。

[3] 欧阳哲生编:《胡适文集》(第六卷)，北京：北京大学出版社，1998。

[4] 曹伯韩、章太炎:《大师的国学课2——常识与概论》,南昌:江西教育出版社,2013。

[5] 翦伯赞:《秦汉史》,北京:北京大学出版社,1999。

[6] 李维武:《王充与中国文化》,贵阳:贵州人民出版社,2000。

[7] 柳诒徵:《中国文化史》(上),上海:上海古籍出版社,2001。

[8] 徐复观:《两汉思想史》第一卷,上海:华东师范大学出版社,2001。

[9] 金春峰:《汉代思想史》,北京:中国社会科学出版社,1987。

[10] 李文东:《"罢黜百家,独尊儒术"与汉武帝的文化政策》,载《许昌师专学报》,1988,第3期。

[11] 李之喆:《是统一,而非专制——重评汉武帝"罢黜百家,独尊儒术"的政策》,载《上海大学学报》,1999,第3期。

[12] 马雪芹:《"罢黜百家,独尊儒术"新解》,载《人文杂志》,1999,第5期。

[13] 刘桂生:《刘桂生学术文化随笔》,北京:中国

［14］ 管怀伦：《汉武帝"罢黜百家，独尊儒术"确有其事——与孙景坛同志商榷》，载《南京社会科学》，1994，总第64期。

［15］ 张分田：《"专制"问题论纲——关于"重建中国思想史知识体系"的若干思考》，载《天津社会科学》，2011，第3期。

［16］ 施治生：《"东方专制主义"概念的历史考察》，载《史学理论研究》，1993，第3期。

［17］〔德〕哈特穆特·凯博：《历史比较研究导论》，赵进中译，北京：北京大学出版社，2009。

［18］ 刘家和：《历史的比较研究与世界历史》，载《北京师范大学学报(社会科学版)》，1996，第5期。

［19］ 范晔撰，李贤等注：《后汉书》（第六册），北京：中华书局，1965。

［20］〔英〕J. B. 伯里：《思想自由史》，周颖如译，北京：商务印书馆，2012。

［21］ 王充撰，陈蒲清点校：《论衡》，长沙：岳麓书社，2015。

［22］〔苏〕阿·阿·彼得洛夫：《王充——中国古代

的唯物主义者和启蒙思想家》,李时译,北京:科学出版社,1956。

[23] 黄中业、陈恩林译注:《论衡选译》,南京:凤凰出版社,2011。

[24] 黄晖:《论衡校释》(四),北京:中华书局,1990。

[25] Barry Baldwin, *Studies in Lucian*, Toronto: A. M. Hakkert Ltd., 1973.

[26] Jones, C. P., *Culture and Society in Lucian*, Cambridge: Harvard University Press, 1986.

[27] Alfred Croiset, Maurice Croiset, *An Abridged History of Greek Literature*, translated by George F. Heffelbower, A. M., London: Macmillan Company, 1904.

[28] 〔俄〕科瓦略夫:《古代罗马史》,王以铸译,上海:上海书店出版社,2007。

[29] 〔英〕马林诺夫斯基:《文化论》,费孝通等译,北京:中国民间文艺出版社,1987。

[30] Lucian, *Zeus Catechized*, in Lucian, *Lucian* Ⅱ, Loeb Classical Library, Cambridge,

Massachusetts: Harvard University Press, 1915.

[31] Lucian, *Demonax*, in Lucian, *Lucian* Ⅰ, Loeb Classical Library, Cambridge, Massachusetts: Harvard University Press, 1913.

[32] 〔古罗马〕琉善:《琉善哲学文选》,罗念生、陈洪文、王焕生等译,北京:商务印书馆,1980。

[33] Lucian, *Zeus Rants*, in Lucian, *Lucian* Ⅱ, Loeb Classical Library, Cambridge, Massachusetts: Harvard University Press, 1915.

[34] Lucian, *Dialogues of the Gods*, in Lucian, *Lucian* Ⅶ, Loeb Classical Library, Cambridge, Massachusetts: Harvard University Press, 1961.

[35] Lucian, *Alexander the False Prophet*, in Lucian, *Lucian* Ⅳ, Loeb Classical Library, Cambridge, Massachusetts: Harvard University Press, 1925.

[36] Lucian, *Lucian*, Vol. Ⅳ, Loeb Classical Library, Cambridge, Massachusetts: Harvard University Press, 1925.

[37] 许慎:《说文解字》,北京:中华书局,1963。

[38] 〔法〕伏尔泰:《风俗论》(上),梁守锵译,北京:

商务印书馆，1994。

[39] 黄晖:《论衡校释》(三)，北京：中华书局，1990。

[40] 永瑢等:《四库全书总目提要》(二)，北京：商务印书馆，1933。

[41] 张鸿、张分田:《王充》，昆明：云南教育出版社，2009。

[42] 邓红:《王充新八论》，北京：中国社会科学出版社，2003。

[43] 黄晖:《论衡校释》(一)，北京：中华书局，1990。

[44] W. L. Hime, *Lucian the Syrian Satirist*, London, New York and Bombay: Longmans, Green, and Co., 1900.

[45] F. G. Allinson, *Lucian, Satirist and Artist*, Boston: Marshall Jones Company, 1926.

[46] Edited by Sarah Iles Johnston, *Ancient Religions*, Cambridge: The Belknap Press of Harvard University Press, 2007.

[47] Don S. Armentrout, "Book Reviews: *The State, Law,*

and Religion: *Pagan Rome*, by Alan Watson", *Church History*, Vol. 63, No. 2.

[48] Edward Gibbon, *History of the Decline and Fall of the Roman Empire*, Penguin Classics, Middlesex: Viking Penguin Inc., 1981.

[49] James B. Rives, "Graeco-Roman Religion in the Roman Empire: Old Assumptions and New Approaches", *Currents in Biblical Research*, Vol. 8, No. 2(2010).

[50] Lucian, *Apology for the "Salaried Posts in Great Houses"*, in Lucian, *Lucian* Ⅵ, Loeb Classical Library, Cambridge, Massachusetts: Harvard University Press, 1959.

[51] Pieter de Villiers, "Interpreting the New Testament in the Light of Pagan Criticisms of Oracles and Prophecies in Greco-Roman Times", *Neotestamentica*, Vol. 33, No. 1(1999).

[52] 〔英〕罗素:《西方哲学史》(上),何兆武、李约瑟译,北京:商务印书馆,1982。

[53] 胡适:《中国哲学史大纲》,北京:商务印书馆,

2011。

[54] 范晔撰，李贤等注：《后汉书》（第九册），北京：中华书局，1965。

[55] 范晔撰，李贤等注：《后汉书》（第七册），北京：中华书局，1965。

[56] 范晔撰，李贤等注：《后汉书》（第四册），北京：中华书局，1965。

[57] 范晔撰，李贤等注：《后汉书》（第六册），北京：中华书局，1965。

[58] 徐斌：《论衡之人——王充传》，杭州：浙江人民出版社，2005。

附 录

Intellectual Liberty during the Han Dynasty:
A Comparative Study of the Religious Criticism of Lucian and Wang Chong

Ni Tengda

I. Discussion on the Policy of Suppressing Intellectuals

The Han Dynasty (206 B.C.-220 A.D.) marked the birth of a policy of thought unity that most, if not all, succeeding dynasties later emulated. It began when Emperor Wu used the Han policy of suppressing intellectual debate to sanction Dong Zhongshu's Cosmological Confucianism as the sole state philosophy. Modern historians disagree about the degree of intellectual liberty that was possible under this draconian policy, which arguably remained in place until the founding of the

Chinese Republic in 1912. Some[1] have argued that this cultural and intellectual autocracy constituted a highly restrictive intellectual environment, while others have offered more liberal interpretations.[2]

---

[1] Wu Yu, "The Confucian-Advocated Danger of the Class System"(吴虞:《儒家主张阶级制度之害》), *New Youth*(《新青年》), vol. 3, no. 4 (1917), p. 3; Chen Duxiu, "The Constitution and Confucianism"(陈独秀:《宪法与孔教》), *New Youth*(《新青年》), vol. 2, no. 3 (1916), p. 2; Ouyang Zhesheng, eds., *Hu Shi Corpus* 6 (欧阳哲生:《胡适文集》), Beijing: Peking University Press, 1998, p. 610; Cao Bohan, Zhang Taiyan, *Class 2 on the Sinology of the Master—Common Sense and Introduction*(曹伯韩、章太炎:《大师的国学课2——常识与概论》), Nanchang: Jiangxi Education Publishing House, 2013, p. 92; Jian Bozan, *Qin-Han History*(翦伯赞:《秦汉史》), Beijing: Peking University Press, 1999, pp. 528–529; Li Weiwu, *Wang Chong and Chinese Culture*(李维武:《王充与中国文化》), Guiyang: Guizhou People's Publishing House, 2000, pp. 18–19.

[2] Liu Yizheng, *History of Chinese Culture* I (柳诒徵:《中国文化史》上), Shanghai: Shanghai Classics Publishing House, 2001, pp. 352–353; Xu Fuguan, *A History of Two Han Dynasty Philosophies* I (徐复观:《两汉思想史》), Shanghai: East China Normal University Press, 2001, p. 193; Jin Chunfeng, *A History of Han Dynasty Philosophies*(金春峰:《汉代思想史》), Beijing: China Social Sciences Publishing House, 1987, p. 201; Li Wendong, "'Ban One Hundred Philosophers and Venerate Confucianism' and the Cultural Policy of Emperor Wu of the Han Dynasty"(李文东:《"罢黜百家,独尊儒术"与汉武帝的文化政策》), *Journal of Xuchang Teachers College*(《许昌师专学报》), no. 3 (1988), p. 79; Li Zhizhe, "Unification but Not Autocracy: Revaluation of

附　录

Most of the aforementioned studies applied a linguistic analytical methodology to original historical texts in search of an answer to this puzzle. However, a glaring conceptual quagmire remains: how do we define "autocracy" in an ancient context? All too often, contemporary discussions of what "autocracy" meant in ancient cultures focus on modern meanings of the term, thus conflating two presumably different concepts. In particular, modern historical studies apply an idea of "autocracy" that is more closely associated

---

Policy: 'Ban One Hundred Philosophers and Venerate Confucianism' of Emperor Wu of the Han Dynasty"(李之喆:《是统一,而非专制——重评汉武帝"罢黜百家,独尊儒术"的政策》), *Journal of Shanghai University*(《上海大学学报》), no. 3, (1999), p. 83; Ma Xueqin, "A New Explanation of 'Ban One Hundred Philosophers and Venerate Confucianism'"(马雪芹:《"罢黜百家,独尊儒术"新解》), *The Journal of Humanities*(《人文杂志》), no. 5(1999), p. 134, 136; Liu Guisheng, *Academic and Cultural Essay of Liu Guisheng*(刘桂生:《刘桂生学术文化随笔》), Peking: China Youth Publishing House, 2000, p. 9; Guan Huailun, "The Real Existence of the Policy 'Ban One Hundred Philosophers and Venerate Confucianism' of Emperor Wu of the Han Dynasty: Discussed with Comrade Sun Jingtan"(管怀伦:《汉武帝"罢黜百家,独尊儒术"确有其事——与孙景坛同志商榷》), *Social Sciences in Nanjing*(《南京社会科学》), no. 64(1994), p. 17.

with Western definitions and connotations.[1] Moreover, no matter the political context, the actual degrees of "autocracy" and "freedom" are relative. Because neither concept has an absolute definition, we need a scale applicable beyond the context of ancient China. Scholars should move beyond traditional boundaries and examine the freedom of thought enjoyed by the intellectuals of ancient China compared to those in other eras of ancient history around the world, rather than assessing the Chinese context in isolation.

---

[1] Zhang Fentian, "The Outline of 'Autocracy': Some Speculation on 'Rebuilding the Knowledge Hierarchy of the History of Chinese Thought'" (张分田:《"专制"问题论纲——关于"重建中国思想史知识体系"的若干思考》), *Tianjin Social Sciences* (《天津社会科学》), no. 3 (2011), p. 120: "The conception of 'autocracy' in modern politics is different from the one in ancient Chinese history...in ancient Chinese, 'autocracy' was always used to describe the powerful officials' power and status." Shi Zhisheng, Guo Fang: "Historical Investigation on the Notion 'Oriental Despotism'" (施治生、郭方:《"东方专制主义"概念的历史考察》), *Historiography Quarterly* (《史学理论研究》), no. 3 (1993), p. 37: "'δεσποτικός' used in Aristotle's work, is an adjective. This word and its adverb form, 'δεσποτικῶς' were both derived from the noun 'δεσπότης'. In etymology, 'δεσπότης' originally meant: 1. patriarch, 2. master of slaves."

Ⅱ. The Religious Criticism of Wang Chong and Lucian

Comparison is an important cognitive approach. Comparative study involves cross-referencing different objects, and its basic function is nothing more than separating similarity from difference. Transverse and synchronic comparison can reveal the similarities and differences of different countries, nations and social groups in the same historical period, thereby potentially demonstrating their epochal features.[1] In the ancient East and West, the respective traditional religions flourished. Before the rise of Christianity, the traditional Greco-Roman religion, centered on the "gods of Olympus", flourished in the Roman Empire. The traditional Chinese religion, which was widespread in the Eastern Han Dynasty, consisted of the activities of *Wu Xi* (巫觋活动) (sorceresses and sorcerers), which descended from the Shang and Zhou dynasties, and the theory of *Chen Wei* (谶

---

[1] Liu Jiahe, "Comparative Study of History and World History"(刘家和：《历史的比较研究与世界历史》), *Journal of Beijing Normal University* (《北京师范大学学报》), no. 5(1996), pp. 46–47.

纬经学), which emerged in the Qin and Han dynasties.

Both Wang Chong(王充)and Lucian were authors with many works to their credit. Wang Chong spent his entire life writing *Lun Heng*(《论衡》). In Fan Ye's(范晔)*Hou Han Shu*(《后汉书》), it is said that Lun Heng consists of eighty-five chapters and over twenty thousand words.[1] Likewise, eighty-two pieces have come down to us under Lucian's name. Both writers presented many thorough discussions about the religious activities of their respective societies. This article intends to adopt a method of comparative study; through a detailed comparison of the critique of divination and prophecy in Wang Chong's and Lucian's works, it can fully grasp the similarities and differences between their religious criticism; by considering their respective backgrounds and individual experiences, we can study the degree of freedom of thought enjoyed by the intellectuals of the Eastern Han Dynasty in China in contrast to those in Rome during the

---

[1] Fan Ye, *Hou Han Shu*(范晔:《后汉书》), vol. Ⅵ, Beijing: Zhonghua Book Company, 1965, p. 1629: "《论衡》八十五篇,二十余万言。"

"reason-free" [1] era in the 2nd century A.D.

Wang Chong (27–97 A.D.), a distinguished thinker during the Eastern Han Dynasty, was born in the third year of Jianwu's reign and passed away in the eighth year of Yongyuan's reign, when the government was quite settled in power. Wang Chong was born into an unpowerful commoner-landlord family, but he eventually "repaired to the capital, where he studied at the academy", and after graduation "took office in the prefecture and was appointed secretary, but in consequence of frequent remonstrances with his superiors, disputes and dissensions with his colleagues, he had to quit the service" [2] and at last "returned to his native land and retired into secluded life as a teacher".[3] During his old age, a carriage was dispatched by the emperor, based on the recommendation of a friend, to secure him an official position, but he

---

[1] J. B. Bury, *A History of Freedom of Thought*, New York : Henry Holt ; London : Williams and Norgate, 1913, p. 21.

[2] Wang Chong, *Lun-Heng* (王充:《论衡》), part Ⅰ, translated by Alfred Forke, London : Luzac & Co., 1907, p. 4.

[3] Fan Ye, *Hou Han Shu* Ⅵ, p. 1629:"后归乡里,屏居教授。"

declined it.[1] Wang Chong is best known for ignoring traditional discipline and the Tao of the sage（非圣无法）and criticizing fallacies（疾虚妄）. He was good at using a rational approach and taking a scientific attitude toward dissecting the ancient Chinese religion. When Wang Chong was recommended to the emperor Hanzhang（汉章帝）, Xie Yiwu（谢夷吾）said of him,"His genius is a natural gift and not acquired by learning. Even Mencius（孟轲）and Sun Ching（孙卿）in former times, or Yang Hsiung（扬雄）, Liu Hsiang（刘歆）, or Sse ma Ch'ien（司马迁）more recently in the Han epoch, could not surpass him."[2]

According to *Zi Ji Pian*（《自纪篇》）, Wang Chong wrote many books, such as *Ji Su*（《讥俗》）, *Jie Yi*（《节义》）, *Zheng Wu*（《政务》）, *Lun Heng* and *Yang Xing*（《养性》）, but the only one that has been handed down to this day is *Lun Heng*. "The *Lun Heng* in its present form has two

---

[1] Wang Chong, *Lun Heng*, punctuated by Chen Puqing（陈蒲清）, Changsha: Yuelu Press, 2015, Preface, pp. 1–2.

[2] Fan Ye, *Hou Han Shu* Ⅵ, p. 1630:"充之天才,非学所加,虽前世孟轲、孙卿、近汉扬雄、刘歆、司马迁,不能过也。"(English version was translated by Alfred Forke, *Lun-Heng* part Ⅰ, 1907, p. 5)

versions (one consists of 30 books, another 35 books), with both comprising 85 chapters. However, of the *Zhao Zhi Pian* (《招致篇》) of chapter 44, we only have the title, not the text, and thus the number of chapters really existing is 84." [1] The chief characteristic of Wang Chong's book is that he based himself in reality and, aiming at the real problems of society, put forward his own thinking and solutions. Wang Chong said in *Zi Ji Pian*:

> "Since Wang Chong deplored the popular feeling, he wrote his Censures on Public Morals, and also lamenting the vain efforts of the emperor's government, which was endeavoring to govern the people, but could not find the right way, nor understand what was required, and mournful and disheartened did not see its course, he wrote the book on government. Furthermore, disgusted with the

---

[1] Huang Zhongye, Chen Enlin, *Selected Translation of Lun-Heng* (黄中业、陈恩林:《论衡选译》), Nanjing: Phoenix Publishing House, 2011, p. 3.

many deceitful books and popular literature devoid of veracity and truthfulness, he composed the Disquisitions." [1] (*Lun Heng*)

Wang Chong's works consist of small essays or chapters and cover a wide range of topics. Wang Chong's spirit of criticizing fallacies is carried out throughout *Lun Heng*, which refuted the false ideas popular at his time. As part of this, the ancient Chinese religion received much attention from Wang Chong.

Lucian (c. 125–180 A.D.), an important scholar who lived during the Roman Empire, and who experienced the second century of a rather stable empire with the *Pax Romana*, "was certainly a leading light of the revival of Greek

---

[1] Huang Hui, *Lun Heng Jiao Shi* (黄晖:《论衡校释》), Ⅳ, Beijing: Zhonghua Book Company, 1990, p. 1194 (English version was translated by Alfred Forke, *Lun-Heng* part Ⅰ, 1907, p. 70): "充既疾俗情,作讥俗之书;又悯人君之政,徒欲治人,不得其宜,不晓其务,愁精苦思,不睹所趋,故作政务之书。又伤伪书俗文多不实诚,故为论衡之书。"

literature known as the Second Sophistic"[1]. About the life of Lucian, little information is recorded. For information about his experience, we mainly make inferences from his work. Lucian's career progressed from sculpture to oratory, which was then pursued by forensic speakers and sophists, and then to literature and satirical writing.[2]

Lucian traveled extensively during his lifetime. He had broad experience and was a man of rich knowledge of the world around him. He based his works on various daily trifles. Like Wang Chong, his works are not masterpieces, but his pamphlets, dialogues, theses and stories involved many aspects of social life in the Roman Empire and discussed citizens' morality, as well as history, pedagogy and aesthetics. Satirical dialogues account for a large proportion of his works. Dialogue was originally a tool of philosophy. However, using dialogue as "hardware"

---

[1] Alison Sharrock, Rhiannon Ash, *Fifty Key Classical Authors*, New York: Routledge, 2002, p. 383.

[2] Barry Baldwin, *Studies in Lucian*, Toronto: Hakkert, 1973, p. 9; C. P. Jones, *Culture and Society in Lucian*, Cambridge: Harvard University Press, 1986, p. 14.

and rhetoric as "software", Lucian employed satirical dialogue, which combined the characteristics of dialogue and rhetoric, to criticize pathological social phenomena. He was different from other intellectuals of his time.[3] His works have a distinct characteristic. They imitated classical works, but—like pouring new wine into an old bottle—they bore the author's original ideas.

Wang Chong and Lucian: one lived in the Eastern Han Dynasty of ancient China, while the other was active in the ancient Roman Empire. The differences in their cultural backgrounds are evident. Although Wang Chong's and Lucian's respective focuses, writing styles, and methodologies of demonstration all differed, a careful comparison of the two writers reveals that they were both good at using rational scientific techniques to analyze ancient religions. Both Wang Chong and Lucian criticized the practice of offering sacrifices to gods and dead men,

---

[3] Alfred Croiset, Maurice Croiset, *An Abridged History of Greek Literature*, translated by George F. Heffelbower, A. M., London: Macmillan Company, 1904, p. 519, 523.

which was common in the ancient world. They each challenged the idea that gods and ghosts were sentient, and they repudiated prophecy. They employed facts and inferences to refute the idea that gods interfered in human affairs, proving that it was of no use to worship deities. Furthermore, they criticized the practice of sacrifice itself and denied the divinity of deities. They insisted that the content of prophecy was obscure, that prophets were not credible and that the activities of prophesying and removing evils should be criticized. They argued against the superstitious hearsay whispered by both ordinary people and intellectuals. Thus, we can see that the two writers often held similar positions regarding religious issues.

Let us take the criticism of prophecy as an example. Living in the world, it is inevitable that people will have contact with human society and with nature. In this process, many factors will be out of people's control, and some things they will be reluctant to accept. As the Polish anthropologist Bronisław Malinowski indicated, when facing the reality of being incapable of practical action, people resort to "magical powers". "Their experience and rationality let them know the limit of their labor and intellect; on the other hand they believed that witchcraft could help them."[1] Therefore, in both the ancient East and the ancient West, people tried to predict the future by means of prophecies and carried out special rituals in an attempt to avoid misfortune and gain advantages in life. These activities, which were an important part of ancient religions, were repudiated by Wang Chong and Lucian.

In Lucian's *Zeus Catechized*, Cyniscus says:

> It does no good to have foreknowledge of future events when people are completely unable to guard against them, unless perhaps you maintain that a man who knows in advance that he is to die by an iron spear-head can

---

[1] Malinowski, *On Culture*, translated by Fei Xiaotong(费孝通等译:《文化论》) Beijing: China Folk Literature and Art Press, 1987, pp. 55–56. (This Chinese version is the only published version because Malinowski's manuscript hasn't yet been issued, and this Chinese translator enjoyed the priority of translating and publishing it.)

escape death by shutting himself up? No, it is impossible, for Fate will take him out hunting and deliver him up to the spear-head.[1]

Lucian expresses a similar opinion in *Demonax*. When he talks about the deeds of the philosopher Demonax, whom he admired very much, he writes:

Again, on seeing a soothsayer make public forecasts for money, [Demonax] said: "I do not see on what ground you claim the fee: if you think you can change destiny in any way, you ask too little, however much you ask; but if everything is to turn out as Heaven has

---

[1] Lucian, *Zeus Catechized*, 12: "Τὸ μὲν ὅλον, ἄχρηστον, ὦ Ζεῦ, προειδέναι τὰμέλλοντα οἷς γε τὸ φυλάξασθαι αὐτὰ παντελῶς ἀδύνατον· εἰ μὴ ἄρα τοῦτο φής, ὡς ὁ προμαθὼν ὅτι ὑπ' αἰχμῆς σιδηρᾶς τεθνήξεται δύναιτ' ἂν ἐκφυγεῖν τὸν θάνατον καθείρξας ἑαυτόν; ἀλλ' ἀδύνατον· ἐξάξει γάρ αὐτόν ἡ Μοῖρα κυνηγετήσοντα καὶ παραδώσει τῇ αἰχμῇ·." The English version of Lucian's works used in this article is quoted from Loeb Classical Library slightly modified.

ordained, what good is your soothsaying?" [1]

Moreover, instead of solving people's problems, in his view, prophecy only brought more confusion. In *Zeus Rants*, when Zeus orders Apollo to predict who will win a debate between two philosophers, Apollo prophecies:

> Hark to the words of the prophet, oracular words of Apollo,
> Touching the shivery strife in which neroes are facing each other.
> Loudly they shout in the battle, and fast-flying words are their weapons;
> Many a blow while the hisses of conflict are ebbing and flowing
> This way and that shall be dealt on the

---

[1] Lucian, *Demonax*, 37: "Καὶ μάντιν δέ ποτε ἰδὼν δημοσίᾳ ἐπὶ μισθῷ μαντευόμενον, Οὐχ ὁρῶ, ἔφη, ἐφ' ὅτῳ τὸν μισθόν ἀπαιτεῖς·τεί μὲν γὰρ ὡς ἀλλάξαι τι δυνάμενος τῶν ἐπικεκλωσμένων, ὀλίγον αἰτεῖς ὁπόσον ἂν αἰτῇς, εἰ ὡς δέδοκται τῷ θεῷ πάντα ἔσται, τί σου δύναται ἡ μαντική."

附 录

crest of the plowtail stubborn;

Yet when the hook-taloned vulture the grasshopper grips in his clutches,

Then shall the rainbearing crows make an end of their cawing forever:

Vict'ry shall go to the mules, and the ass will rejoice in his offspring![1]

This piece of prophecy rambles all the way through and does not provide any useful information. Thus Momus, as Lucian's mouthpiece in the story, says: "How can I [stop laughing], Zeus, when the oracle is so clear and

---

[1] Lucian, *Zeus Rants*, 31:
"Κέκλυτε μαντιπόλου τόδε θέσφατον Ἀπόλλωνος
ἀμφ' ἔριδος κρυερῆς, τὴν ἄνερες ἐστήσαντο
ὀξυβόαι, μύθοισι κορυσσόμενοι πυκινοῖσι.
πολλὰ γὰρ ἔνθα καὶ ἔνθα μόθου ἑτεραλκέϊ κλωγμῷ
ταρφέος ἄκρα κόρυμβα καταπλήσσουσιν ἐχέτλης.
ἀλλ' ὅταν αἰγυπιὸς γαμψώνυχος ἀκρίδα μάρψῃ,
δὴ τότε λοίσθιον ὀμβροφόροι κλάγξουσι κορῶναι.
νίκη δ' ἡμιόνων, ὁ δ' ὄνος θοὰ τέκνα κορύψει."

manifest?"[1] And by "clear and manifest", he means: "The prophecy says as plainly as you please that this fellow is a humbug and that you who believe in him are pack-asses and mules, without as much sense as grasshoppers."[2] Later in the story, Lucian mentions the tragedy of Croesus,[3] and through the words of the Epicurean philosopher Damis he ridicules the Oracle of Delphi and censures the ambiguity of Apollo's prophecy, which, as Lucian says, is made double, like Hermes' face, alike whether you look at the

---

[1] Ibid., 31 : "Καὶ πῶς δυνατόν, ὦ Ζεῦ, ἐφ'οὕτω σαφεῖ καὶ προδήλῳ τῷ χρησμῷ."

[2] Ibid., 31 : "φησὶ γὰρ τὸ λόγιον οὑτωσί διαρρήδην γόητα μὲν εἶναι τοῦτον, ὑμᾶς δὲ ὄνους κανθηλίους νὴ Δία καὶ ἡμιόνους, τοὺς πιστεύοντας αὐτῷ, οὐδ' ὅσον αἱ ἀκρίδες τὸν νοῦν ἔχοντας."

[3] Croesus was a king of Lydia who prepared a campaign against Cyrus the Great of Persia. Before setting out, he turned to the Oracle of Delphi to inquire whether he should pursue this campaign. The oracle answered that if Croesus attacked the Persians, he would destroy a great empire. Croesus thought the great empire would be Persia, but it turned out that the empire destroyed by the war was Croesus's own. Cf. Luo Niansheng, Chen Hongwen, Wang Huansheng, Feng Wenhua, *Selection of Lucian's Philosophy Works* (罗念生、陈洪文、王焕生、冯文华译:《琉善哲学文选》), Beijing : Commercial Press, 1980, p. 176, n. 2.

front or the back.[1] These passages demonstrate Lucian's criticism of the fuzziness and fraudulence of prophecy. Furthermore, in his *Dialogues of the Gods*, he satirizes Apollo, god of the sun, himself as dispensing prophecies for others all day but knowing nothing about his own future.[2]

As he continued to criticize prophecy, another important target for Lucian was the false prophet Alexander. In *Alexander the False Prophet* Lucian recounts the charlatan Alexander's misdeeds, unravels several of his frauds, and quotes many instances to prove that the alleged prophecies were ridiculous. For example, when some Rutilianus asks whose soul he has inherited, the reply he receives is as follows:

> Peleus's son wert thou at the first; thereafter Menander,
> Then what thou seemest now, and

---

[1] Lucian, *Zeus Rants*, 43.

[2] Lucian, *Dialogues of the Gods*, 18(16), 244.

hereafter shalt turn to a sunbeam.

Four score seasons of life shall be given thee over a hundred.[1]

However, this Rutilianus dies at the age of seventy. In another example, someone enquires whom he should employ as his young son's tutor. Alexander prophesies: "Be it Pythagoras; aye, and the good bard, [2] master of warfare." [3] However, after a few days the boy dies unexpectedly, and the lie of the prophecy is exposed by the facts. Lucian's work reveals that the real acts of the prophet who was so popular among people at that time are "lying, trickery, perjury, and malice; facile, audacious, venturesome, diligent in the execution of its schemes,

---

[1] Lucian, *Alexander the False Prophet*, 34: "Πρῶτον πηλείδης ἐγένου, μετὰ ταῦτα Μένανδρος, εἶθ' ὃς νῦν φαίνῃ, μετὰ δ' ἔσσεαι ἡλιὰς ἀκτίς, ζήσεις δ' ὀγδώκοντ' ἐπὶ τοῖς ἕκατον λυκάβαντας."

[2] "The good bard" is Homer. Cf. Luo Niansheng, Chen Hongwen, Wang Huansheng, Feng Wenhua, *Selection of Lucian's Philosophy Works*, p. 235, n. 1.

[3] Lucian, *Alexander the False Prophet*, 33: "Πυθαγόρην πολέμων τε διάκτορον ἐσθλὸν ἀοιδόν."

plausible, convincing, masking as good, and wearing an appearance absolutely opposite to its purpose" [1]. Lucian's satirical assault on Alexander is unsparing and biting; Lucian claims that it would be more difficult to enumerate all the tricks and frauds of the impostor Alexander of Abonutichus than to cleanse the Augean stable completely. In Lucian's view, Alexander is more brutal than a robber, and even recounting his story is shameful.[2]

Lucian also indicates in his work that the serious consequences of "prophecy" include not only the waste of money and manpower but even taking lives and endangering national security. Alexander of Abonutichus incited Severianus to attack Armenia, thus leading to

---

[1] Ibid., 4: "ὅλως γὰρ ἐπινόησόν μοι καὶ τῷ λογισμῷ διατύπωσον ποικιλωτάτην τινὰ ψυχῆς κρᾶσιν ἐκ ψεύδους καὶ δόλων καὶ ἐπιορκιῶν καὶ κακοτεχνιῶν συγκειμένην, ῥᾳδίαν, τολμηράν, παράβολον, φιλόπονον ἐξεργάσασθαι τὰ νοηθέντα, καὶ πιθανήν καὶ ἀξιόπιστον καὶ ὑποκριτικὴν τοῦ βελτίονος καὶ τῷ ἐναντιωτάτῳ τῆς βουλήσεως ἐοικυῖαν."

[2] Ibid., 1–2.

the total destruction of Severianus himself and his army.[1] On another occasion when emperor Marcus Aurelius was busy preparing to wage a battle against the Marcomanni and Quadi in the war in Germany, [2] Alexander issued the following prophecy:

> Into the pools of the Ister, the stream that from Zeus taketh issue,
> Hurl, I command you, a pair of Cybele's faithful attendants,
> Beasts[3] that dwell on the mountains, and all that the Indian climate
> Yieldeth of flower and herb that is

---

[1] Ibid., 27. The Parthians had been interfering with the succession to the throne in Armenia. Severianus, Roman governor of Cappadocia, entered Armenia with a small force in 161 and was defeated. (Lucian, *Lucian*, Vol. IV, Loeb Classical Library, Cambridge, MA: Harvard University Press, 1925, 213, n.2)

[2] Ibid., 48.

[3] "Beasts" here means "lions". Cf. Luo Niansheng, Chen Hongwen, Wang Huansheng, Feng Wenhua, *Selection of Lucian's Philosophy Works*, p.241, n.4.

fragrant; amain there shall follow

　　Victory and great glory, and welcome peace in their footsteps.[1]

However, after the Romans had done all that was asked by the prophecy and thrown sacred herbs and lions into the Ister, the lions swam ashore and accessed the field of the enemy. Considering them to be dogs or wolves, the barbarians beat them to death. The next thing beaten was the Roman army.[2]

Facing up to his own failed prophecy, Alexander tried to conceal his failure and did not blush to exonerate himself by quoting the story of Croesus, saying that the oracle only foretold the emergence of victory and peace, not whether the Romans or barbarians should have it. These two ridiculous prophecies caused great suffering and losses

---

[1] Lucian, *Alexander the False Prophet*, 48 : "Ἐς δίνας Ἴστροιο διιπετέος ποταμοῖοἐσβαλέειν κέλομαι δοιοὺς Κυβέλης θεράποντας, θῆρας ὀριτρεφέας, καὶ ὅσα τρέφει Ἰνδικὸς ἀήρἄνθεα καὶ βοτάνας εὐώδεας· αὐτίκα δ᾽ ἔσταινίκη καὶ μέγα κῦδος ἅμ᾽ εἰρήνῃ ἐρατεινῇ."

[2] Ibid., 48.

to the Roman Empire.

In addition to the harmful direct effects detailed above, Lucian also exposes the hidden effects of superstitions on politics. For example, *in Alexander the False Prophet* he says :

> In opening and reading the forwarded scrolls, if [Alexander] found anything dangerous and venturesome in the questions, he would keep them himself and not send them back, in order to hold the senders in subjection and all but in slavery because of their fear, since they remembered what it was that they had asked. You understand what questions are likely to be put by men who are rich and very powerful.[1]

---

[1] Ibid., 32 : "λύων γὰρ τὰ πεπεμμένα βιβλία καὶ ἀναγιγνώσκων, εἴ τι εὕροι ἐπισφαλὲς καὶ παρακεκινδυνευμένον ἐν ταῖς ἐρωτήσεσιν, κατεῖχεν αὐτὸς καὶ οὐκ ἀπέπεμπεν, ὡς ὑποχειρίους καὶ μονονουχί δούλους διὰ τὸ δέος ἔχοι τοὺς πεπομφότας, μεμνημένους οἷα. ἦν ἃ

Thus it can be seen that, as the speakers for gods, the organizers of superstitions might possess, and administer, the secrets of the ruling class. The control of these secrets was equivalent to the control of the people, which meant that there was an invisible hand backstage, quietly influencing the destiny of the empire. Lucian's works clearly expose this hidden peril.

Shuo Wen Jie Zi (《说文解字》) says "'占' consists of '卜' and '口', which means observing an omen" ("占,视兆也,从卜口"), [1] which shows that divination is essentially the action of acquiring an omen. As Voltaire says, "Les divinations, les augures, étaient des espèces d'oracles, & sont, je crois, d'une plus haute antiquité ; car il falait bien des" [2]. *Bushi* (卜筮), an ancient divining

---

ἤροντο. συνίης δὲ οἵας εἰκός τοὺς πλουσίους καὶ μέγα δυναμένους τὰς πύστεις πυνθάνεσθαι."

[1] Xu Shen, *Shuo Wen Jie Zi* (许慎:《说文解字》), Beijing : Zhonghua Book Company, 1963, p.70.

[2] Voltaire, *Essai sur les Moeurs et L'Esprit des Nations et sur les Principaux* vol. 1. Lausanne : François Grasset et Cie, 1770, p.140 ; i. e. "observing an omen and foretelling the future are also divination, and I think they're even much older."

activity, was very popular during the Han Dynasty. Like Lucian, Wang Chong believed that divination should be repudiated—so much so that in *Bu Shi*(《卜筮》)he criticized superstitious activities involving divination. *Bushi*, as discussed by Wang Chong, was quite similar to the prophesying that ancient Romans solicited from divinities. The ancient Chinese people also asked questions to their divinities, especially Heaven(天)and Earth(地). *Bu* (卜)is the act of the diviner asking Heaven a question; *shi*(筮)is the act of the diviner asking Earth a question. Milfoil(蓍草)and tortoise shells(龟甲)were common tools for divination. The people of ancient China believed that Heaven and Earth answered the diviners' questions through the signs that the tortoise shells and milfoil manifested. Wang Chong points out that, "As a matter of fact, diviners do not ask Heaven and Earth, nor have weeds or tortoises spiritual qualities" [1]. In other words,

---

[1] Huang Hui, *Lun Heng Jiao Shi* Ⅲ, p. 998(English version was translated by Alfred Forke, *Lun-Heng* part Ⅰ, 1907, p. 182):"如实论之,卜筮不问天地,蓍龟未必神灵。"

milfoil and tortoise shells were not always reliable, so *bushi* failed to achieve the aim of asking questions of the divinities.

Wang Chong, recalling the dialogue between Confucius and his student Zi Lu (子路), puts forward the idea that milfoil and tortoise shells, having no practical effect, are used in divination only because of the implied meanings of *shi* (蓍, longevity) and *gui* (龟, harbor): "In order to elucidate doubtful things, one must ask the old and the aged." [1] In combination, the phrase means that if you have a question, you should consult an elder. From this, we can conclude that milfoil and tortoise shells possess no supernatural power, so they are not actually suitable for asking questions to Heaven and Earth. Wang Chong also points out that Heaven and Earth are tangible and capable of motion, which means that, to the people of ancient China, they were alive. In light of the principle of human activity, provided that a question relates to a living

---

[1] Ibid., p. 999 (English version was translated by Alfred Forke, *Lun-Heng* part Ⅰ, 1907, p. 182): "明狐疑之事，当问耆旧也。"

soul, one should then ask a living soul. How can we obtain answers to questions asked of an animate Heaven and Earth by virtue of inanimate milfoil and tortoise shells? Moreover, if it is true that *bushi* is the way to ask Heaven and Earth a question, and an omen is their response, reality will not be like that:

> It is usual among men to answer, when asked, and not to reply, unless there be any question. Should anybody knock at other people's door without any reason, not wishing anything, or make a useless discourse in their presence, without asking their opinion, the master of the house would laugh, but not reply, or he would become angry, and not give an answer. Now, let a diviner perforate a tortoise shell in sheer play, or sort the milfoil for nothing, and thus mock Heaven and Earth, he would obtain omens and signs all the same. Would Heaven and Earth then

reply indiscriminately? Or let a man revile Heaven, while divining by shells, or beat the Earth, while drawing the lots which is the height of impiety, he would obtain omens and signs nevertheless. If omens and signs are the spirit of Heaven and Earth, why do they not extinguish the fire of the diviner, burn his hand, shake his fingers, disturb his signs, strike his body with painful diseases, and cause his blood to freeze and to boil, instead of still showing him omens and sending signs? Do Heaven and Earth not fear the bother, and not disdain to take this trouble?[1]

---

[1] Ibid., p. 1001 (English version was translated by Alfred Forke, *Lun-Heng* part Ⅰ, 1907, pp. 184-185): "人道，相问则对，不问不应。无求，空扣人之门；无问，虚辨人之前，则主人笑而不应，或怒而不对。试使卜筮之人，空钻龟而卜，虚揲蓍而筮，戏弄天地，亦得兆数，天地妄应乎？又试使人骂天而卜，欧地而筮，无道至甚，亦得兆数。苟谓兆数天地之神，何不灭其火，灼其手，振其指而乱其数，使之身体疾痛，血气凑硌？而犹为之见兆出数，何天地之不惮劳，用心不恶也？"

That is to say, regardless of whether diviners are allowed to divine aimlessly or abuse Heaven and Earth in the process, any divination will obtain a result. There can never be a case of no omen being received, or the diviner being punished.

Secondly, Wang Chong demonstrates that divination is impractical. If someone has a question for Heaven, then Heaven is asked directly, but how can anyone figure out whether Heaven has a body—particularly ears? If Heaven has, how could Heaven hear human questions, when its body and ears are so far away? If Heaven has not, then Heaven could not answer any questions at all. Furthermore, due to natural law, it is not possible for Heaven to answer human questions consciously.

Wang Chong also frequently mentions the following analogy: a human being is as small compared to Heaven as a louse is to a human being. Thus, human questions cannot reach the ear of Heaven due to the remoteness and magnitude of Heaven. Some people claim that:

附 录

Man carries the fluid[1] of Heaven and Earth in his bosom. This fluid in the body is the mind, I dare say. When man is going to divine by weeds and shells, he puts questions to the milfoil and the tortoise. The replies which he hears with his ears, his mind regards like its own thoughts. From the depth of the bosom and the stomach the mind hears the explanation. Thus, when the tortoise is cut to pieces and the divining stalks grasped, omens and signs appear.[2]

This means that human beings all harbor the air of Heaven and Earth, which is divinity, and thus divinity can perceive people's questions by virtue of people's

---

[1] I.e. air(气), Alfred Forke translated it as "fluid".
[2] Huang Hui, *Lun Heng Jiao Shi* Ⅲ, p. 1000 (English version was translated by Alfred Forke, *Lun-Heng part* Ⅰ, 1907, p. 183.):"人怀天地之气。天地之气,在形体之中,神明是矣。人将卜筮,告令蓍龟,则神以耳闻口言。若己思念,神明从胸腹之中闻知其旨,故钻龟揲蓍,兆见数著。"

mouths, ears, chests and abdomens and then show the appropriate omen with the tortoise shells and milfoil. Regarding this opinion, Wang Chong retorted that, following this logic, the results of divination would never run counter to the anticipation in people's hearts because:

> Now, the thoughts are one's own spirit, and that which causes the omens and signs is also one's spirit. In the bosom, the spirit of a body becomes the mental power, and outside the bosom, omens and signs. It is as if a man enters a house, and sits down or goes out through the door. The walking and sitting make no difference in his ideas, and entering or issuing does not change his feelings.[1]

In other words, thinking should be in accordance with

---

[1] Ibid., p. 1000 (English version was translated by Alfred Forke, *Lun-Heng* part Ⅰ, 1907, pp. 183–184.): "夫思虑者,己之神也;为兆数者,亦己之神也。一身之神,在胸中为思虑,在胸外为兆数,犹人入户而坐,出门而行也,行坐不异意,出入不易情。"

action. Provided that the people's thoughts reflect those of the divinities and that omens are the concrete expression of the divinities' ideas, then omens should be consistent with people's expectations.

In both ancient Rome and ancient China, omens had an impact on important state affairs. *Chen Wei* (谶纬), which was criticized by Wang Chong, is the most typical one of those omens. *Wei* (纬) is an interpretation of Confucian classics; *Chen* (谶) is the prophecy of divinities. In *Sikuquanshu zongmu tiyao* (《四库全书总目提要》), it is said:

> Confucians often talk about *Chen Wei*. Actually, *Chen* is *Chen* itself, while *Wei* is *Wei* itself. They are different from each other. *Chen* is a type of enigmatic language which tries to predict the future... *Wei* are branches of Confucian classics and expound the

meanings of Confucian classics.[1]

As scholars Zhang Hong(张鸿) and Zhang Fentian (张分田) said: "Strictly speaking, *Chen* and *Wei* are from different categories. However, *Wei* must make up omens in *Chen* to look more sacred; in turn, *Chen Yu*(谶语, a statement of *Chen Wei*) can be more convincing depending on Confucian classics, so it is hard to definitely distinguish between them because of their gradual integration."[2]

Chen Wei was very popular during the Han Dynasty, so much so that almost everyone—from the emperor and court officials to the common people—believed in that practice.

"The core of *Chen Wei* was the political thoughts mainly discussing the order or disorder of the world, the

---

[1] Yong Rong, *Sikuquanshu Zongmu Tiyao*(永瑢:《四库全书总目提要》), vol. 2. Beijing: Commercial Press, 1933, p. 62: "案儒者多称'谶纬', 其实谶自谶, 纬自纬, 非一类也。谶者, 诡为隐语, 预决吉凶;……纬者, 经之支流, 衍及旁义。"

[2] Zhang Hong, Zhang Fentian, *Wang Chong* (张鸿、张分田:《王充》), Kunming: Yunnan Educational Press, 2009, p. 94.

rise or decline of the country, the gain or loss of politics, the separation or reunion of monarch and subject and so on... Because *Weishu*(纬书) and *Chen Wen* mainly dabbled in the most sensitive issues on the legality of political power, they received the extensive attention of the court and the masses." [1] For instance, some *Chen* said that Confucius had predicted before he died that "I know not what sort of fellow, styling himself the First Emperor of *Ch'in*, comes to my hall, squats on my bed, and turns my clothes topsy-turvy. After arriving at *Sha-ch'iu* he will die" [2]. In another example, one omen went as follows: "*Ch'in* will be ruined by *Hu*." [3] All of the above are typical *Chen Yu*. The former predicted the appearance and death of the First Qin Emperor (259B.C.–210B.C.); the latter foretold that the

---

[1] Ibid., p. 94.

[2] Huang Hui, *Lun Heng Jiao Shi* Ⅳ, p. 1069 (English version was translated by Alfred Forke, *Lun-Heng* part Ⅱ, 1962, p. 114):"不知何一男子,自谓秦始皇,上我之堂,踞我之床,颠倒我的衣裳,至沙丘而亡。"

[3] Ibid., p. 1070 (English version was translated by Alfred Forke, *Lun-Heng* part Ⅱ, 1962, pp. 114–115):"亡秦者,胡也。"

保守抑或包容

Second Qin Emperor, Hu Hai(胡亥, 230B.C.–207B.C.) would ruin the country. Wang Chong criticized the contents of *Chen Yu* carefully.[1] He said in *Shi Zhi*(《实知》):

> Prophecy books and other mystic writings see from afar what has not yet come to pass; they are aware of what is going to happen in the future, which, for the time being, is still a void and wrapped in darkness. Their knowledge is instantaneous, supernatural, and passing all understanding.[2]

Wang Chong alleged that a majority of the sayings in *Chen Wei* were sheer fabrications or deliberate distortions of earlier remarks and were thus absolutely not credible.[3]

---

[1] Wang Chong criticized the contents of *Chen Yu* in *Shi Zhi* (《实知》).

[2] Huang Hui, *Lun Heng Jiao Shi* Ⅳ, p. 1072. (English version was translated by Alfred Forke, *Lun-Heng* part Ⅱ, 1962, p. 117): "谶书秘文，远见未然，空虚暗昧，豫睹未有，达闻暂见，卓谲怪神，若非庸口所能言。"

[3] Zhang Hong, Zhang Fentian, *Wang Chong*, p. 97.

Like Lucian, Wang Chong extends the focus of his discussion to prophets. He said, "There are many people discoursing on divination, but very few who understand its real meaning" [1], which means that of the many people who talk about divination, those who are capable of interpreting omens are quite rare. Omens appear when divinations are conducted using tortoise shells and milfoil; however, the results of divination are less easy to get because diviners know nothing about how to explain the omens. Wang Chong cites two examples of divinations, one conducted when King Wu overthrew the Shang Dynasty(武王伐纣)and the other when Lu was going to attack Yue(鲁将伐越), [2] to demonstrate:

---

[1] Huang Hui, *Lun Heng Jiao Shi* Ⅲ, p. 1003 (English version was translated by Alfred Forke, *Lun-Heng* part Ⅰ, 1907, p.187):"世人言卜筮者多,得实诚者寡。"

[2] Wang Chong, *Lun-Heng*, part Ⅰ, Alfred Forke, trans., p. 188:"When King Wu of Zhou destroyed the Shang Dynasty, he encountered unlucky omens but ended in victory. In the Spring and Autumn Period, when Lu was going to attack Yue, the diviners by milfoil gave their verdict to the effect that the tripod had broken its leg. Tse Kung(子贡)explained this as evil, because the tripod had its leg broken, and for moving on people need legs. Confucius, on the other hand, explained it as lucky, saying, 'The people of Yue are living on the water; to reach them one requires

> In Chou there were many persons who could give a straightforward interpretation, such as Tse Kung (子贡), but very few gifted with the same subtle reasoning power, such as Confucius. Consequently, upon viewing an unusual omen, they were unable to catch the meaning.[1]

In other words, most people during the Zhou Dynasty could only explain omens literally, just like Tse Kung; Confucius' outstanding ability to demonstrate results was rare. If diviners fail to provide accurate explanations, how can they then convince people to believe that divination can provide them with the right answers?

Finally, if, as Lucian says, the fate of human beings is unchangeable, what is the point of divination? Wang

---

boats, not legs.' Therefore he called it lucky. At last, Lu invaded Yue and finally defeated it."

[1] Huang Hui, *Lun Heng Jiao Shi* Ⅲ, p. 1005 (English version was translated by Alfred Forke, *Lun-Heng* part Ⅰ, 1907, p. 188.): "周多子贡直占之知,寡若孔子诡论之材,故睹非常之兆,不能审也。"

Chong, adhering to his opinion on natural determination, claims that human beings are made from the "air" (气) deriving from Heaven and Earth and have different "fates" (命) determined by the diverse thicknesses of the air they were bestowed at birth. Fate determines people's wealth or poverty and all their encounters, both good and bad, so "human beings must or have to succumb"[1]. Just as Wang Chong's *Ming Lu* (《命禄》) said:

> Man's success as well as his troubles depend upon destiny. It determines his life and his death, and the length of his span, and it likewise provides for his rank and his wealth. From the princes and dukes downwards to the commoners, and from the sages and worthies down to the illiterate people, all those who have a head and eyes, and blood in their veins, each and every one possess their

---

[1] Deng Hong, *Eight New Theories about Wang Chong* (邓红:《王充新八论》), Beijing: China Social Sciences Publishing House, 2003, p. 64.

own destiny.[1]

If all things are predestined, what is the point of consulting Heaven and Earth? Even if people obtain an answer, what can they do? Fate is constrained and cannot be changed; likewise, one's fortune cannot be altered, no matter how hard people strive to do so. Therefore, it is futile to predict, or even try to change, things. Instead, it is better to learn from clever people to accept reality, thus acquiring a tranquil and accepting mindset.[2]

A comparison of Wang Chong's and Lucian's writings indicates that they share the view that prophecies are useless. They both note the obscurity and ambiguity of prophecies and the unreliability of prophets, criticize almost all prophecies that have an impact on state or political affairs, and demonstrate the meaninglessness of

---

[1] Huang Hui, *Lun Heng Jiao Shi* I, p. 20 (English version was translated by Alfred Forke, *Lun-Heng* part I, 1907, p. 144.):"凡人遇偶及遭累害，皆由命也。有死生寿夭之命，亦有贵贱贫富之命。自王公逮庶人，圣贤及下愚，凡有首目之类，含血之属，莫不有命。"

[2] Ibid., p. 20:"命则不可勉，时则不可力，知者归之于天，故坦荡恬忽。"

divination and prophecy due to the unchangeable nature of fate.

In the same way, we can prove that there are many similarities between them in regard to the propositions that sacrificing to the gods has no effect, that people's spirits vanish as soon as their bodies decay, that *Wu Zhu* [巫祝, in ancient China, people dealing with affairs related to ghosts and gods were called *Wu* (巫), and the singing of eulogies when sacrificing were called *Zhu* (祝)] are incapable of reversing the course of events, that superstition and hearsay are ridiculous and make fools of people, and so on. All of these points reflect that these two eminent thinkers harbored strong rational spirits and clear critical attitudes toward religion.

Ⅲ. Rejection Does Not Mean Persecution

Both Lucian and Wang Chong lived in a time when beliefs and politics mingled profoundly. "Lucian happened to be born at a period when superstition was widespread and miracles were fashionable...The leading men of the age were devout. The emperor, Marcus Aurelius, thought life would not be worth living without gods; Fronto prayed daily for the recovery of the Empress Faustina when she was ill; Pliny the Younger built two temples; Dion Chrysostom, Plutarch and Epictetus were theists; and all of them believed firmly in the intervention of the gods in human affairs."[1]

As Francis G. Allinson said, "In this brilliant Age of the Antonines superstitions, home-made and oriental, flourished under the genial sunlight of the Roman Empire alongside the noble philosophy inculcated by Imperial example"[2]. In the second century, the Roman Empire put a premium on traditional religion. Ancient Roman religion was deeply intertwined with the political world.[3] "The job of the gods was to protect and strengthen the state, and the priests were public officials who performed

---

[1] W. L. Hime, *Lucian the Syrian Satirist*, London, New York and Bombay: Longmans, Green, and Co., 1900, pp. 27-28.

[2] F. G. Allinson, *Lucian, Satirist and Artist*, Boston: Marshall Jones Company, 1926, p. 89.

[3] S. I. Johnston, eds., *Ancient Religions*, Cambridge. MA: Belknap, 2007, p. 228.

the rites that the gods wished or required." [1] As Gibbon says, "They (Roman governors) knew and valued the advantages of religion, as it is connected with civil government. They encouraged the public festivals, which humanize the manners of the people. They managed the arts of divination, as a convenient instrument of policy" [2]. Therefore, religious belief was the core problem attracting the attention of the ruling class of Rome.[3] However, Lucian mercilessly criticized traditional Greco-Roman religion. In terms of content, he attacked the practice of sacrifice, criticized prophecy, and satirized divinities; in his approach, he applied the tactics of ridicule and satire, and he was equipped with all types of philosophical theories as instruments. Fallacies had no escape from his

---

[1] D. S. Armentrout, "Book Reviews: *The State, Law, and Religion: Pagan Rome*, by Alan Watson", *Church History*, vol. 63, no. 2 (Jun., 1994), p. 250.

[2] E. Gibbon, *History of the Decline and Fall of the Roman Empire* vol. I, London: Penguin Books Ltd., 1994, p. 59.

[3] J. B. Rives, "Graeco-Roman Religion in the Roman Empire: Old Assumptions and New Approaches", http://cbi.sagepub.com/content/8/2/240, accessed December 9, 2014, p. 249.

pen. Despite his attacks on the instrument of policy, he was not subjected to political persecution. He travelled around delivering speeches, built up a good relationship with the upper class of Rome, and even held a post in Egypt. He earned a rather high salary, was proud of his vocation, and was filled with expectations regarding his future development. [1]

J. B. Bury once called the time in which Lucian lived the "reason-free" era: "The general rule of Roman policy was to tolerate throughout the Empire all religions and all opinions. Blasphemy was not punished. The principle was expressed in the maxim of the Emperor Tiberius: 'If the gods are insulted, let them see to it themselves.'" [2] The Roman Empire rarely placed restrictions on speech. In fact, this criticism of Greco-Roman traditional religion "should be seen as part of a wider movement that can be traced as far back as the Pre-Socratic philosophers

---

[1] Lucian, *Apology for the "Salaried Posts in Great Houses"*, 12.

[2] J. B. Bury, *A History of Freedom of Thought*, p. 40.

in Greece".[1] From the Pre-Socratic period to Aristotle, philosophy and traditional religion seem to have been incompatible. The critique of traditional religion comes from the idea that philosophy belongs to one of the two categories of spiritual classification that ran parallel in ancient Greece: "There were, in fact, two tendencies in Greece, one passionate, religious, mystical, otherworldly, the other cheerful, empirical, rationalistic, and interested in acquiring knowledge of a diversity of facts. Herodotus represents this latter tendency; so do the earliest Ionian philosophers; so, up to a point, does Aristotle." [2] Hence, ancient philosophers would not be faithful disciples of traditional religions. For instance, one of the Pre-Socratic philosophers, Protagoras, clearly questioned the existence of god in *On the Gods*: "With regard to the gods, I cannot feel sure either that they are or that they are

---

[1] Pieter de Villiers, "Interpreting the New Testament in the Light of Pagan Criticisms of Oracles and Prophecies in Greco-Roman Times", *Neotestamentica*, vol. 33, no. 1 (1999), p. 48.

[2] B. Russell, *History of Western Philosophy*, London: George Allen & Unwin Ltd., 1946, Taylor & Francis E-Library edition, p. 47.

not, nor what they are like in figure ; for there are many things that hinder sure knowledge, the obscurity of the subject and the shortness of human life." [1] In the classical period, Aristotle's god was very different from that of the Greco-Roman religion : "He deemed that god is eternal and perfect, is pure thought, happiness and completely self-dependent actuality...God is pure form without any matter." [2] "It is clear then from what has been said that there is a substance which is eternal and unmovable and separate from sensible things. It has been shown that this substance cannot have any magnitude, but is without parts and indivisible...However, it has also been shown that it is impassive and unalterable." [3] Epicurus, although he believed that god existed, argued that god did not interfere with human beings[4] and was against the world's

---

[1] Ibid., p. 108.

[2] B. Russell, *History of Western Philosophy*, translated by Zhang Zuocheng(张作成), Beijing : Beijing Publishing House, 2007, p. 42.

[3] B. Russell, *History of Western Philosophy*, 1946, p. 202.

[4] Ibid., p. 284.

obsession with witchcraft and divination.[1] By the time of the Roman Empire, "the harsh criticism of Lucian was not the occasional brave remark of a daring individual"[2]. Cicero also rejected divination, which was not free from falsehood and trickery, in his *De Divinatione* 1.58.[3] In addition, he used the observation that the Delphic Oracle was no longer functioning as an argument against oracles in *De Divinatione* 2.57.[4]

On all these counts, we can see that the disrespect of intellectuals to Greco-Roman religion did not begin with Lucian. This has been the case in the West since the classical age. Most philosophers participated in traditional sacrificial activities while rejecting traditional beliefs.[5] However, the impiety did not bring them serious

---

[1] Ibid., p. 285.

[2] Pieter de Villiers, "Interpreting the New Testament in the Light of Pagan Criticisms of Oracles and Prophecies in Greco-Roman Times", p. 40.

[3] Ibid., p. 42.

[4] Ibid., p. 44.

[5] Because traditional religion, which was inevitable, permeated every aspect of daily life in ancient times. About the detailed discussion, cf. my

persecution. In addition, the emperor of Rome in the age of Lucian was Marcus Aurelius (A.D. 121–180), who devoted himself to Stoic virtue. In other words, Lucian lived in an age when the emperor himself was a philosopher. Marcus Aurelius was a great thinker himself; he knew the difference between thought and action, and understood that it was possible to acquire philosophical beliefs and engage in daily religious activities simultaneously. Under these cultural circumstances, intellectuals enjoyed considerable freedom of thought, so it is no wonder that scholars such as Lucian became famous during that time.

The comparison with Lucian shows us that Wang Chong harbored the same rational critical spirit: both objected to the practice of sacrificing to divinities and ghosts, criticized divination, and condemned hearsay and taboo. Hu Shi(胡适)says that there were roughly three essential tenets of ancient Chinese religions:

---

article: "Review and Reflection: Gods in Lucian's Views", *Journal of Beijing Normal University*, no. 2, (2015), p. 89.

One, having a Heaven with consciousness who could be capable of rewarding the good and punishing the evil; two, worshipping a variety of superstitions, for example, sacrificing to Heaven, the earth, the sun, the moon, mountains, rivers and the like; three, being superstitious about ghosts and divinities, believing that sacrificing and supporting them is necessary because the dead are capable of determining weal and woe. These superstitions deserve to be the state religions, with the emperor (天子) as leader in ancient China.[1]

Wang Chong carried out a comprehensive and sustained critique of worshipping Heaven as a personified god (人格神). However, actually, Wang Chong was not the pioneer of this type of criticism. Similar reflections have a

---

[1] Hu Shi, *An Outline of Philosophic History of China* (胡适:《中国哲学史大纲》), Beijing: Commercial Press, 2011, p. 319.

long tradition in the history of ancient Chinese philosophy. As early as the Spring and Autumn Period, Lao Zi(老子)put forward the idea of *Tiandao Buren*(天道不仁)against the concept of the old *Tian Dao*(天道, the Dao of Heaven), which was to think of Heaven as a conscious and temperamental master of all things.[1] With Xun Zi(荀子), the argument for the concept of "Heaven as unconscious" reached its height. Xun Zi not only used Lao Zi's *Tiandao Buren* to amend the Confucian concept of a conscious Heaven but also averted the negative effects of Lao Zi and Zhuang Zi's(庄子)concept of Heaven, which led people to fatalism and pessimism. Xun Zi put *Tian Dao* aside and paid attention to human power, encouraging people to conquer the Dao of Heaven and make use of it.[2]

The thoughts of philosophers from the Han to Jin dynasties were all based on the ancient philosophy that preceded the Han Dynasty.[3] The emergence of Wang

---

[1] Ibid., p.42.

[2] Ibid., p.250.

[3] Ibid., Introduction, p.5.

Chong's thought was a result of the previous achievements' influence. Thus, he claimed the assertion that there is no interaction between Heaven and Man. However, the formation of a person's thoughts also has much to do with his historical background. Lao Zi was against the old Dao of Heaven because he was born in a time when the whole world was in chaos, and seeing people killed, families destroyed and states subjugated he felt that, if there were a conscious Heaven, these types of disaster would never happen.[1] In the same way, the reason Wang Chong opposed *Tianren ganying*(天人感应, the interaction between Heaven and Man) was the rapid expansion of the hereditary landlords of the Eastern Han Dynasty: they "monopolized privileges and annexed land, which not only led to conflicts with farmers but also aroused the strong dissatisfaction of the common landlords and brewed a new social crisis"[2]. In this situation, the rulers of the Eastern Han Dynasty tried to promote the theory of *Tianren ganying* proposed by

---

[1] Ibid., p. 41.

[2] Wang Chong, *Lun Heng*, punctuated by Chen Puqing, 2015, Preface, p. 1.

Dong Zhongshu (董仲舒) to strengthen their rule. Under the guidance of this theory, religious superstition and *Chen Wei* were popular, and people were duped and confused. Wang Chong was deeply worried and thought he should "aim at truth and dislike all wild speculations"[1] (事实疾妄) and criticize the above phenomenon.

The *Tianren ganying* served as a philosophical foundation for the monarch, as well as a crucial instrument for controlling subjects and unifying thinking. The government strongly supported various divination practices and sacrifices. The idea of the emperor as ruler was closely connected with the superstitious concept of worshipping Heaven as a personified god:

> If the social structure, including the whole body of customs and opinions, is associated intimately with religious belief and is supposed to be under divine patronage,

---

[1] Wang Chong, *Lun-Heng*, part I, translated by Alfred Forke, 1907, p. 91.

> criticism of the social order savours of impiety, while criticism of the religious belief is a direct challenge to the wrath of supernatural powers.[1]

In turn, challenging the punishments and condemnations handed down by the gods was essentially criticism of prevailing ideas, and the work of Wang Chong was a direct challenge to these punishments and condemnations. Wang Chong thereby questioned the ruling philosophy of the ruler himself in the Eastern Han Dynasty.

Most people think that ancient China, as a strongly unified society, undertook to ban all other schools of philosophers and venerate Confucianism(罢黜百家,独尊儒术); cultural autocracy took root following the Han Dynasty, under which intellectuals suffered severe persecution.[2] Stories about Yin Min (尹敏), Huan Tan(桓谭), and others are often brought up as examples. However, these events should be considered

---

[1] J. B. Bury, *A History of Freedom of Thought*, pp. 9–10.
[2] Zhang Hong, Zhang Fentian, *Wang Chong*, p. 92.

from the perspective of politics rather than intellectual thought. The *Hou Han Shu*(《后汉书》)records:

> Because Yin Min was educated in Confucian classics, the emperor ordered him to proofread and sort out the *Tuchen* (图谶, a book of prophecy in Confucian classics) and expurgate the *tuchen*, which were made up by Cui Fa for Wang Mang. Yin Min responded: "*Chenshu* (谶书, i.e., 图谶) were not written by the sage and contained many characteristics of wrongly written words, which like remarks were widely popularized among common people, and which readers might bungle after." The emperor did not adopt his advice. Thus, Yin Min took advantage of the lacuna in *tuchen* and added that the character "君" without "口" would be the prime minister of the Han Dynasty.[1] The emperor wondered

---

[1] The character "君" without "口" is "尹," which is Yin Min's family name.

at it and asked him about the reason. Yin Min answered: "I found that our predecessors added to and expurgated the *tuchen*, so I ventured to anchor my hope on it too." The emperor thought he could not be more wrong. Though he escaped punishment, Yin Min has not taken important positions for such reasons.[1]

Yin Min, who had previously expressed his objection to *Chen Wei* clearly before the emperor, challenged and falsified *Chenshu* without being punished; his failure to be further promoted was due to his refusal to conform with the attitudes of the central government. It was because of his being implicated with Zhou Lyu(周虑)that Yin Min was removed from office and put into prison: "In the fifth year of Yongping's

---

[1] Fan Ye, *Hou Han Shu* IX, p. 2558:"帝以敏博通经记，令校图谶，使阙去崔发所为王莽着录次比。敏对曰，'谶书非圣人所作，其中多近鄙别字，颇类世俗之辞，恐疑误后生。'帝不纳。敏因其阙文增之曰：'君无口，为汉辅。'帝见而怪之，召敏问其故。敏对曰：'臣见前人增损图书，敢不自量，窃幸万一。'帝深非之，虽竟不罪，而亦以此沉滞。"

reign, a summons was issued to arrest a man named Zhou Lyu. Zhou Lyu was very famous and obtained on well with Yin Min. Yin Min was thus not protected from the impact and was released from his position." [1] This shows that political issues were far more critical than ideological issues for the rulers of the Eastern Han Dynasty.

Huan Tan, who objected to *Chen Wei*, was nearly sentenced to death, not because he followed heterogeneous thinking but because he publicly objected to the government's cultural policy, namely by directly challenging the power and policy of the emperor. At the beginning of the Eastern Han Dynasty, emperor Guangwu （光武帝）, under the name of Liu Xiu（刘秀）, promoted *Chen Wei* to stabilize his reign. In *Hou Han Shu*, it is said that he "was adept at Chen" （善谶）[2]. The contradiction between Huan Tan and Liu Xiu lay in their political ideas, which were revealed not long after Liu Xiu took the throne：

---

[1] Ibid., p. 2559：" 永平五年,诏书捕男子周虑。虑素有名称,而善于敏,敏坐系免官。"

[2] Fan Ye, *Hou Han Shu* Ⅶ, p. 1911.

"After [he] acceded to the throne, *Shizu* (i.e., Liu Xiu) summoned Huan Tan and was about to offer him an office, but later he was not satisfied with Huan Tan's opinions on government affairs and didn't appoint him." [1] Thus we can see that the political ideas that Huan Tan proposed when he had just taken office were inconsistent with the emperor's ideas. He later submitted written statements twice to the emperor, in which he advised frankly and courageously that the emperor should not believe in *Chen Yu* and that not enough funds and rewards were used for military purposes. This behavior made the emperor even more displeased with him. Later on, when discussing where an altar (灵台) should be placed, the emperor asked Huan Tan for his suggestions on using *Chen Yu* to determine the position, which was probably an intentional provocation. Liu Xiu, aware of Huan Tan's view on the subject, still challenged him to set forth the proposition that *Chenshu* was non-classical, intending to behead him on the pretext of "ignoring

---

[1] Fan Ye, *Hou Han Shu* Ⅳ, p. 956: "世祖即位，征待诏，上书言事失旨，不用。"

traditional discipline and the Tao of the sage"[1]. Conflicts such as this reflect the increasingly intense tension between politicians and scholars when it came to imperial and administrative authority, rather than the restrictions the emperor imposed on intellectual thought and the extremely rare freedom of thought that the government granted to intellectuals.

Meanwhile, despite his actions and thoughts, Wang Chong suffered no persecution based on his rational spirit and radical writing. Though his official career was full of twists and turns, Wang Chong did dabble in officialdom and took political office four times, which shows that the ruling class did not give up on him. Moreover, Wang Chong involved himself in teaching and running schools to disseminate his thinking. The first time he went into seclusion voluntarily, he "returned to his native land and retired into secluded life as a teacher"[2]. In teaching his students, he likewise sought to realize the spirit of

---

[1] Ibid., p. 961:"桓谭非圣无法。"

[2] Fan Ye, *Hou Han Shu* VI, p. 1629.

"pursuing truth and criticizing fallacies"[1] in his life, devoting himself to teaching his students true and useful things and clarifying many "assertions of fallacy"[2]. What is more notable is that Wang Chong unexpectedly received a *tezhaogongchezheng* (特诏公车征, a summons issued by the emperor, who dispatched a special carriage to take the summoned to the palace) issued by emperor Hanzhang (汉章帝) in 88 A.D. and was offered a higher position than ever before, namely, being in office around the emperor at a time when *Lun Heng* had been completed and was starting to attract attention. Of course, the comfortable life Wang Chong finally achieved may have had something to do with his writing *Qi Shi Pian* (《齐世篇》), *Xuan Han Pian*[3] (《宣汉篇》), which further illustrates that rulers in the Han Dynasty valued political standpoints more than a controlled intellectual atmosphere. There was

---

[1] Xu Bin, *The One Who Wrote "Lun Heng": Biography of Wang Chong* (徐斌:《论衡之人——王充传》), Hangzhou: Zhejiang People's Publishing House, 2005, p. 116: "实事疾妄。"

[2] Ibid., p. 117: "虚妄之语。"

[3] Articles that celebrated the reign of the Han Dynasty.

no integrated centralized monarchy by which the Hundred Schools of Thought in the pre-Qin period could be contested without being persecuted ; the fact that under the policies of strengthening the central government, banning the hundred philosophers and strengthening Confucianism in the Eastern Han Dynasty, Wang Chong could still escape unscathed further shows that the regime of his time did not impose a harsh crackdown on intellectuals.

IV. Conclusion

In conclusion, both Lucian and Wang Chong criticized the traditional religion valued by their respective ruling classes and attacked the instruments on which the implementation of official policy depended, but neither suffered direct persecution from the government. They regained their official posts in their later years, when their respective ideas had spread and become accepted. Unexpectedly, the intellectual environment of Wang Chong in the Eastern Han Dynasty was similar to that of Lucian in the "reason-free" era of Rome. The similarities between the two thinkers indicate that the cultural policy of the Eastern

Han Dynasty did not suppress public intellectuals or their work, as previous scholars have asserted, but on the contrary, gave them a measure of freedom by which they could promote their thoughts.

Bibliography

[1] Wu Yu, "The Confucian-Advocated Danger of the Class System" (吴虞:《儒家主张阶级制度之害》), *New Youth* (《新青年》), vol. 3, no. 4 (1917).

[2] Chen Duxiu, "The Constitution and Confucianism" (陈独秀:《宪法与孔教》), *New Youth* (《新青年》), vol. 2, no. 3 (1916).

[3] Ouyang Zhesheng, eds., *Hu Shi Corpus* 6 (欧阳哲生编:《胡适文集》), Beijing: Peking University Press, 1998.

[4] Cao Bohan, Zhang Taiyan, *Class 2 on the Sinology of the Master—Common Sense and Introduction* (曹伯韩、章太炎:《大师的国学课 2——常识与概论》), Nanchang: Jiangxi Education Publishing House,

2013.

[5] Jian Bozan, *Qin-Han History*(翦伯赞:《秦汉史》), Beijing : Peking University Press, 1999.

[6] Li Weiwu, *Wang Chong and Chinese Culture*(李维武:《王充与中国文化》), Guiyang : Guizhou People's Publishing House, 2000.

[7] Liu Yizheng, *History of Chinese Culture* Ⅰ(柳诒徵:《中国文化史》上), Shanghai : Shanghai Classics Publishing House, 2001.

[8] Xu Fuguan, *A History of Two Han Dynasty Philosophies* Ⅰ(徐复观:《两汉思想史》), Shanghai : East China Normal University Press, 2001.

[9] Jin Chunfeng, *A History of Han Dynasty Philosophies*(金春峰:《汉代思想史》), Beijing : China Social Sciences Publishing House, 1987.

[10] Li Wendong, " 'Ban One Hundred Philosophers and Venerate Confucianism' and the Cultural Policy of Emperor Wu of the Han Dynasty"(李文东:《"罢黜百家,独尊儒术"与汉武帝的文化政策》), *Journal of Xuchang Teachers College*(《许昌师专

学报》), no. 3 (1988).

[11] Li Zhizhe, "Unification but Not Autocracy: Revaluation of Policy: 'Ban One Hundred Philosophers and Venerate Confucianism' of Emperor Wu of the Han Dynasty"(李之喆:《是统一,而非专制——重评汉武帝"罢黜百家,独尊儒术"的政策》), *Journal of Shanghai University*(《上海大学学报》), no. 3, (1999).

[12] Ma Xueqin, "A New Explanation of 'Ban One Hundred Philosophers and Venerate Confucianism'"(马雪芹:《"罢黜百家,独尊儒术"新解》), *The Journal of Humanities*(《人文杂志》), no. 5 (1999).

[13] Liu Guisheng, *Academic and Cultural Essay of Liu Guisheng*(刘桂生:《刘桂生学术文化随笔》), Peking: China Youth Publishing House, 2000.

[14] Guan Huailun, "The Real Existence of the Policy 'Ban One Hundred Philosophers and Venerate Confucianism' of Emperor Wu of the Han Dynasty: Discussed with Comrade Sun Jingtan"(管怀伦:《汉

武帝"罢黜百家,独尊儒术"确有其事——与孙景坛同志商榷》), *Social Sciences in Nanjing*(《南京社会科学》), no. 64(1994).

[15] Zhang Fentian, "The Outline of 'Autocracy': Some Speculation on 'Rebuilding the Knowledge Hierarchy of the History of Chinese Thought'"(张分田:《"专制"问题论纲——关于"重建中国思想史知识体系"的若干思考》), *Tianjin Social Sciences*(《天津社会科学》), no. 3(2011).

[16] Shi Zhisheng, Guo Fang: "Historical Investigation on the Notion 'Oriental Despotism'"(施治生、郭方:《"东方专制主义"概念的历史考察》), *Historiography Quarterly*(《史学理论研究》), no. 3(1993).

[17] Liu Jiahe, "Comparative Study of History and World History"(刘家和:《历史的比较研究与世界历史》), *Journal of Beijing Normal University*(《北京师范大学学报》), no. 5(1996).

[18] Fan Ye, *Hou Han Shu*(范晔:《后汉书》), Beijing: Zhonghua Book Company, 1965.

[19] J. B. Bury, *A History of Freedom of Thought*,

New York : Henry Holt ; London : Williams and Norgate, 1913.

[20] Wang Chong, *Lun-Heng*(王充:《论衡》), part I, translated by Alfred Forke, London : Luzac & Co., 1907.

[21] Wang Chong, *Lun Heng*, punctuated by Chen Puqing(陈蒲清), Changsha : Yuelu Press, 2015.

[22] Huang Zhongye, Chen Enlin, *Selected Translation of Lun-Heng*(黄中业、陈恩林:《论衡选译》), Nanjing : Phoenix Publishing House, 2011.

[23] Huang Hui, *Lun Heng Jiao Shi*(黄晖:《论衡校释》), Beijing : Zhonghua Book Company, 1990.

[24] Barry Baldwin, *Studies in Lucian*, Toronto : A. M. Hakkert Ltd., 1973.

[25] Alison Sharrock, Rhiannon Ash, *Fifty Key Classical Authors*, New York : Routledge, 2002.

[26] C. P. Jones, *Culture and Society in Lucian*, Cambridge : Harvard University Press, 1986.

[27] Alfred Croiset, Maurice Croiset, *An Abridged History of Greek Literature*, translated by George

F. Heffelbower, A. M., London: Macmillan Company, 1904.

[28] Malinowski, *On Culture*, translated by Fei Xiaotong (费孝通等译:《文化论》) Beijing: China Folk Literature and Art Press, 1987.

[29] Lucian, *Zeus Catechized*, in Lucian, *Lucian* Ⅱ, Loeb Classical Library, Cambridge, Massachusetts: Harvard University Press, 1915.

[30] Lucian, *Demonax*, in Lucian, *Lucian* Ⅰ, Loeb Classical Library, Cambridge, Massachusetts: Harvard University Press, 1913.

[31] Lucian, *Zeus Rants*, in Lucian, *Lucian* Ⅱ, Loeb Classical Library, Cambridge, Massachusetts: Harvard University Press, 1915.

[32] Luo Niansheng, Chen Hongwen, Wang Huansheng, Feng Wenhua, *Selection of Lucian's Philosophy Works* (罗念生、陈洪文、王焕生、冯文华译:《琉善哲学文选》), Beijing: Commercial Press, 1980.

[33] Lucian, *Dialogues of the Gods*, in Lucian,

Lucian Ⅷ, Loeb Classical Library, Cambridge, Massachusetts: Harvard University Press, 1961.

[34] Lucian, *Alexander the False Prophet*, in Lucian, *Lucian* Ⅳ, Loeb Classical Library, Cambridge, Massachusetts: Harvard University Press, 1925.

[35] Xu Shen, *Shuo Wen Jie Zi*(许慎:《说文解字》), Beijing: Zhonghua Book Company, 1963.

[36] Voltaire, *Essai sur les Moeurs et L'Esprit des Nations et sur les Principaux* vol.1. Lausanne: François Grasset et Cie, 1770.

[37] Yong Rong, *Sikuquanshu Zongmu Tiyao*(永瑢:《四库全书总目提要》), vol. 2, Beijing: Commercial Press, 1933.

[38] Zhang Hong, Zhang Fentian, *Wang Chong*(张鸿、张分田:《王充》), Kunming: Yunnan Educational Press, 2009.

[39] Deng Hong, *Eight New Theories about Wang Chong*(邓红:《王充新八论》), Beijing: China Social Sciences Publishing House, 2003.

[40] W. L. Hime, *Lucian the Syrian Satirist*, London,

New York and Bombay : Longmans, Green, and Co., 1900.

[41] F. G. Allinson, *Lucian, Satirist and Artist*, Boston : Marshall Jones Company, 1926.

[42] S. I. Johnston, eds., *Ancient Religions*, Cambridge. MA : Belknap, 2007.

[43] D. S. Armentrout, "Book Reviews : *The State, Law, and Religion, Pagan Rome*, by Alan Watson", *Church History*, vol. 63, no. 2 (Jun., 1994).

[44] E. Gibbon, *History of the Decline and Fall of the Roman Empire* vol. I , London : Penguin Books Ltd., 1994.

[45] J. B. Rives, "Graeco-Roman Religion in the Roman Empire : Old Assumptions and New Approaches", http : //cbi.sagepub.com/content/8/2/240, accessed December 9, 2014.

[46] Lucian, *Apology for the "Salaried Posts in Great Houses"*, in Lucian, *Lucian* VI, Loeb Classical Library, Cambridge, Massachusetts : Harvard

University Press, 1959.

[47] Pieter de Villiers, "Interpreting the New Testament in the Light of Pagan Criticisms of Oracles and Prophecies in Greco-Roman Times", *Neotestamentica*, vol. 33, no. 1(1999).

[48] B. Russell, *History of Western Philosophy*, London: George Allen & Unwin Ltd., 1946, Taylor & Francis E-Library edition.

[49] B. Russell, *History of Western Philosophy*, translated by Zhang Zuocheng(张作成), Beijing: Beijing Publishing House, 2007.

[50] Hu Shi, *An Outline of Philosophic History of China*(胡适:《中国哲学史大纲》), Beijing: Commercial Press, 2011.

[51] Xu Bin, *The One Who Wrote "Lun Heng": Biography of Wang Chong*(徐斌:《论衡之人——王充传》), Hangzhou: Zhejiang People's Publishing House, 2005.